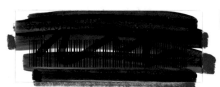

Higher Education in Rural America

SERVING THE ADULT LEARNER

Higher Education in Rural America

SERVING THE ADULT LEARNER

Douglas M. Treadway

College Entrance Examination Board
New York • 1984

The College Board is a nonprofit, membership organization that provides tests and other educational services for students, schools, and colleges. The membership is composed of more than 2,500 colleges, schools, school systems, and education associations. Representatives of the members serve on the Board of Trustees and advisory councils and committees that consider the programs of the College Board, and participate in the determination of its policies and activities.

The Office of Adult Learning Services (OALS) of the College Board conducts activities to improve adults' access to postsecondary education. The major goals of the office are to provide new programs, training, and publications to support the transition of adults to and from education; help institutions strengthen their capabilities in lifelong education; develop the skills of professionals who serve adults; assemble and disseminate information about adult learning; and advance knowledge in the field of adult learning. To meet these goals, the office offers advisory services, technical assistance, and training workshops. It also produces publications and develops new products.

Printed in the United States of America.

Copies of this book may be ordered from College Board Publications, Box 886, New York, New York 10101. The price is $8.95.

Editorial inquiries concerning this book should be directed to: Editorial Office, The College Board, 888 Seventh Avenue, New York, New York 10106.

ISBN No. 0-87447-176-1

Contents

Foreword   vii
Preface   ix

1 • Introduction 1

Rural Communities and Needs   3
Scale and Size of Community   7
Isolation   8
Cultural Homogeneity within the Community   9
Agricultural Tradition   10
Participation in Adult Education   11
Educational Needs of Rural Adults   11

2 • Types of Rural Education Programs 17

GED and ABE Programs   18
Occupational Training   19
Counseling and Information Programs   20
Economic Development   21
Adult Education   22
Special Rural Populations   23
Campus-Based Programs Focusing on Rural Needs   23
Industry-Based Training   25
New Delivery Systems   25
Independent and Individualized Study Programs   28
Integrated Systems Approaches   28

3 • Program Development and Strategies 31

Gaining Access to People in Their Communities   32
Developing Local Involvement   33
Determining Needs and Relating to Institutional Mission   35
Fostering Interinstitutional Collaboration   37
Facilitating Communications: Learners, Staff, and Institution   39
Use of Creative Strategies   41
Characteristics of Effective Outreach Programs   45

4 • Issues for Postsecondary Institutions 47

Relating Institutional Mission to Rural Clientele   47
Establishing Delivery Systems   49
Institutional Policies and Administration   54

5 • Issues for National and State Policy 57

Issues at the National Level   59
Issues for State Policies   62
A Rural Postsecondary Action Agenda   64

References   65
Practitioners' Library   68
Books of Interest from the College Board   71

Foreword

The College Board's Office of Adult Learning Services (OALS) has as its major purpose the improvement of adults' access to postsecondary education. The challenge for OALS is an immense one: adult learning continues to rise dramatically. At present, more than 35 percent of all college students are over 25 years old. It is expected that by 1990 half of all college students will be adult learners.

Many adult learners live in rural America: in 1981, six million participated in adult education, according to the United States Bureau of the Census. Their participation accounted for almost 30 percent of all adult learning that took place in the United States. Like their urban counterparts, adults living in rural areas want education that relates to their immediate needs and has practical consequences for them. Unlike their urban cousins, rural adult learners are usually older and have had fewer years of formal education; they also face more problems and barriers that restrict their access to postsecondary education. In rural America there are fewer education institutions, opportunities, and resources than in urban areas. In addition, access is limited because of poor public transportation, the adult learner's geographic isolation, and the lack of a comprehensive education delivery system. Meeting the educational needs of this group in the next decade will be critical. Institutions of higher education, therefore, will want to respond to the challenges offered by the special needs of this group.

As there have been few systematic surveys and little collection of national data on the educational needs of rural adults, Douglas Treadway's book serves as a particularly important contribution to the field. He addresses the problems by identifying needs, citing examples of effective rural education programs, and raises the isssues that need to be discussed by educators and public policymakers. Treadway's analysis and recommendations for action can help educators bring higher education to more adult learners living in rural America.

Carol B. Aslanian
Director, Office of
Adult Learning Services
The College Board

Preface

This book is an overview of the "state of the art" in outreach programs for adults in rural areas. Although I have not attempted a thorough review of this field, I have tried, from one college's experience and viewpoint, to highlight major issues, opportunities, and some proven strategies. It is hoped that this will further stimulate efforts of educators to learn from one another and for government officials to look more closely at the need actively to support activities that make quality postsecondary learning opportunities more fully accessible to the rural populations of the nation.

Higher Education in Rural America is an outgrowth of a project sponsored by the United States Department of Education, the Fund for the Improvement of Postsecondary Education (FIPSE). The project was conducted over the period 1979–82 at Eastern Oregon State College (EOSC), in La Grande, Oregon. The purpose was to develop a comprehensive delivery system of college-level learning opportunities for place-bound adults in rural communities.

More than 40 different agencies, schools, libraries, and institutions have cooperated with EOSC in the development of its outreach efforts. To the extent that the goals were met, they are shared accomplishments of these many service providers and also of the more than 4,000 rural adult learners who have been participants and consultants. I particularly want to acknowledge Marylee Newman and Catherine Rolsinzki, the FIPSE project officers who provided assistance to EOSC, and Rodney Briggs, past president of EOSC; his advocacy and support were vital to the success of the project.

I also would like to express my appreciation and thanks for the help and advice received from Werner Bruecher, Martha Butt, Mary Emery, Roger McCannon, Winnifred Voelker, and Margery Walker, all of whom took time to review the book in its early stages.

Preparation of the final manuscript was undertaken by the Office of Adult Learning Services (OALS) of the College Board. Special thanks go to Deborah Kahane, assistant director of OALS, who was responsible for the overall coordination of the book.

Douglas M. Treadway

Dean, Division of Continuing Education
and Regional Programs
Eastern Oregon State College
La Grande, Oregon

Introduction

A farm magazine carried a cartoon that showed a farmer's pickup truck crashed into a four-door sedan where a country road crossed a highway. The driver of the sedan, dressed in a business suit, was being confronted by a farmer in coveralls. The farmer was saying, "What do you mean *I* didn't see you? Everyone from around these parts knows I come out on this road about this time every day!"

There is little question that rural people have viewpoints about their lives, needs, and communities that are not necessarily always understood or appreciated by people from the outside.

It has not always been this way in the United States. During the first 150 years of our history, America was mostly a rural nation. Six out of every ten people still lived in rural places at the turn of this century. Since then there have been many changes, including the mechanization of agriculture, improvements in communications and transportation systems, industrialization, and overall economic and social change. Having gone through the past 50 years, in which city and suburban living had come to dominate the attention of the growing nation, there is, however, an apparent transition taking place.

In the final quarter of this century the living patterns are again undergoing a change—a shifting back to rural awareness, but for new-found reasons. A survey by the rural sociologist Edwin A. Carpenter in 1977 found that 75 percent of Americans prefer to live in a town with a population under 50,000 but would like the small town to be within 30 miles of a city. Only 19 percent surveyed wanted to be more than 30 miles away from a city.

In 1979 the Carter administration published a policy statement on small-community and rural development. The introduction to that statement reads in part as follows:

> As we enter our third century, the living patterns and preferences of Americans are shifting (again). These shifts between urban and rural are occurring in the context of an extraordinary diversity within rural America itself. The diversity is mirrored in the variety of our rural areas—areas that take such divergent forms as a New England coastal fishing village, a Midwest farm community, a mining town in Appalachia, a ranching area in the Rocky Mountains, a settlement of tenant farmers in the Mississippi Delta, a pueblo in the Southwest, a Southern town in transition to becoming a metropolitan center, and a small Western town experiencing "boom growth" from energy development.

Rural America was rediscovered during the decade of the 1970s. Industries in search of clean environments for their employees; retired people seeking solace from the big cities; the back-to-nature movement that saw many urban-oriented people of all ages experimenting with farming, outdoor pursuits, and folk lore; and other factors contributed to the rediscovery. The population trend of the nation actually reversed itself, as more growth was found in the nonmetropolitan areas than in the cities. Demographers have labeled this "rural turnaround"—the net United States migration was *into* rural areas, not away from them.

The population shifts are producing changes in rural life. Some sociologists predict that by the year 2000 there will be little meaning to the word *rural* as a descriptor of people's lives (in contrast with *urban*). In other words, rural society is being urbanized. Changes in employment patterns, education, health care, social mores, and ethnic mixes are occurring in rural communities largely owing to outside influences.

No doubt the most significant aspect of the new demographics is that fewer than 2 million of the 22 million rural Americans who are gainfully employed now labor in agriculture, forestry, or fisheries. "We have a new distribution of people upon the land," notes H. E. Conklin, "one that has never existed before in the history of the human race. It is a pattern in which non-farm people live in the country, far outnumbering farmers in most rural towns."

As rural distinctions gradually disappear, the need for education, awareness, and resources to cope with change becomes dramatic. The goals of full employment, economic development, and good health care cannot be met without equal emphasis on the goal of lifelong learning and equal educational opportunity. Whether rural people live on reservations, in mining towns, or on wheat farms, those people must be empowered through education to have a say in the directions their lives take under the outside influence of social and economic change. There are many problems facing rural communities in their determination to maintain their long-enjoyed quality of life and environment. There are many needs, as a result, for ongoing learning opportunities to equip adequately the rural citizenry to cope with their problems as well as to enjoy the benefits of learning for personal and social development.

In the first part of the twentieth century, the nation responded to its rural population's education needs through creation of the land grant universities and colleges of teacher education (normal schools). Today there are new challenges that are far more encompassing and demanding. Community colleges and other community-based organizations are in the forefront. State colleges and universities, private colleges,and many other education providers are looking into how they can play a part in meeting the challenge. This book takes a look at the needs in rural communities, some of the programs now in place, and some of the issues that need to be faced in relation to institutional, state, and federal policies, as we move into the twenty-first century and a new world of lifelong learning for all citizens.

Rural Communities and Needs

According to the U.S. Census Bureau, *rural* means residence on a farm, in open countryside, or in areas of fewer than 2,500 residents. In 1980, 28.8 percent of the United States population was classified as "rural" by this definition. In Figure 1 the trends in population are shown from 1880 to 1980.

Whereas the total number of people living in small towns is now increasing, the percentage of the total U.S. population living on a *farm* continues to decrease. In 1880, 43.8 percent of the total population lived on a farm; in

FIGURE 1. Trends in United States Population

Year	Total U.S. population (millions)	Rural population (millions)
1980	50,156	36,971 (73.7%)
1910	91,972	49,349 (53.7%)
1930	122,775	53,820 (43.8%)
1950	150,697	61,770 (41.0%)
1960	179,323	53,765 (30.0%)
1970	203,212	55,887 (26.5%)
1980	206,505	59,539 (28.8%)

From Rosenfeld 1981 and 1980 census data.

FIGURE 2. U.S. Standard Metropolitan Statistical Areas, 1970–80

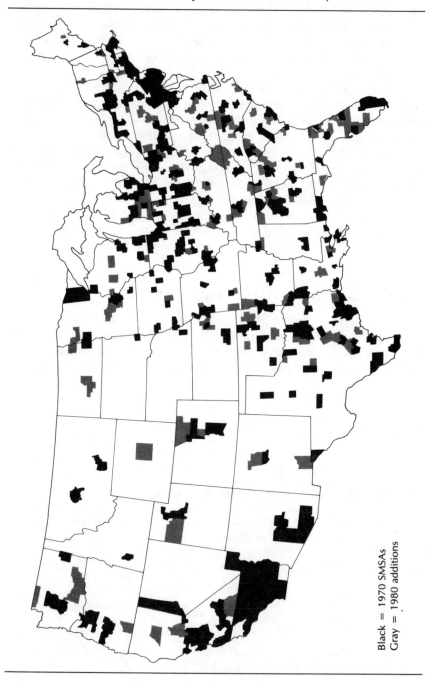

Black = 1970 SMSAs
Gray = 1980 additions

1980, only 3.4 percent. As agriculture continues to mechanize and be less labor intensive, this percentage will continue to decline. By the year 2000 only 1 to 2 percent of the population will be needed to produce all the agricultural products the country requires.

An expanded definition of *rural* now in use by the government is "residence outside a Standard Metropolitan Statistical Area (SMSA)," a term for areas that include a city with at least 50,000 inhabitants. In Figure 2 the SMSAS of the United States are shown as they were designated in 1970 and revised in 1980.

One difference between SMSAS and nonmetropolitan areas that influences the needs for education is the age distribution of the population. As a result of the out-migration of youth (due largely to lack of economic opportunities) and to the in-migration of the elderly to rural retirement areas, rural communities tend to be older. In nonmetropolitan areas 38 percent of the population is over age 44, while in metropolitan areas 31 percent is over 44.

As a result of the in-migration of retired people, together with relocations of industry and other factors, nonmetropolitan areas are changing at a faster rate than metropolitan areas, except in the South, where the rate of change is almost the same (see Figure 3).

In general, it can be said that in comparison with residents of metropolitan communities, residents of rural communities have the following characteristics.

- older
- fewer years of formal education
- decreasing number of farmers
- lower taxes (but receive fewer public services)

People in rural communities tend to be more alike than people in large cities, but rural communities across the country tend to be more unlike each other than do large cities across the country. The entire rural population does not operate as, and cannot be treated as, a single polity in matters of education, economic development, social and health needs, and so on. However, despite the wide cultural and economic variations, there are dominant demographic and economic conditions associated with being designated rural. These include the following.

- scale and size of community
- isolation
- cultural homogeneity within the community
- an agricultural tradition

Further consideration of these conditions and their implications for adult education will now be considered.

FIGURE 3. Rate of Change in Regional Population Growth, 1970–80

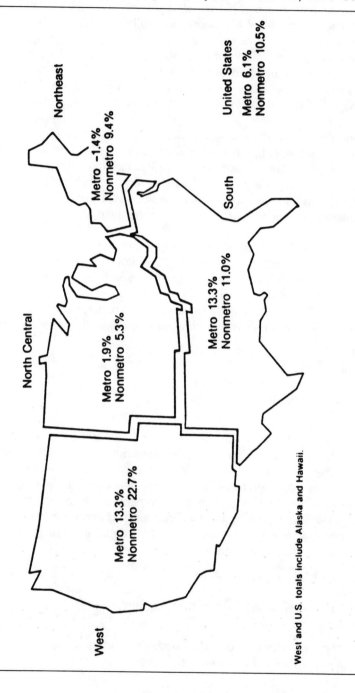

Northeast
Metro −1.4%
Nonmetro 9.4%

United States
Metro 6.1%
Nonmetro 10.5%

South
Metro 13.3%
Nonmetro 11.0%

North Central
Metro 1.9%
Nonmetro 5.3%

West
Metro 13.3%
Nonmetro 22.7%

West and U.S. totals include Alaska and Hawaii.

Scale and size of community

Small communities share a common denominator in that social interactions and communications span all major areas of life, whereas in urban areas such communication tends to be fragmented by separate relations in work, residence, church, clubs, and organizations. In small towns people work, worship, socialize, and go to town meetings with the same people they do business with at banks and stores. In urban areas people most often do not socialize with their coworkers or people they do business with. The social intimacy of the small town is an asset in most instances, although in some instances the lack of social privacy can be a disadvantage.

Size of the community of origin of an individual (more so than city of current residence) has been found to be a reliable predictor of social attitudes. For example, Glenn (1977) found that city residents from rural backgrounds retain their rural attitudes. He also found that although age and education are the most useful social indicators of behavior and attitudes, size of community of origin is as useful as family income, occupation prestige, and other common indicators.

There may be higher satisfaction among citizens of small communities with their community than has been found in social research of urban areas. A survey of 27 small towns in Iowa found that most of the people interviewed liked their community (Goudy, 1977). The most important criteria for satisfaction in the small community were strong primary group relations, participation in local affairs, pride in civic affairs, shared decision making, heterogeneous population, and people committed to community upkeep. Some researchers feel that dissatisfied people simply do not remain in small towns—the dissatisfied leave.

Resources for education and public services in rural areas are constrained by diseconomies of scale. For example, small schools are unable to offer both the wide range of educational opportunities available to urban youth and the "extras" of urban schools—swimming pools, well-equipped auditoriums, and physics labs. Moreover, programs requiring a large investment, such as vocational education, are even more restricted by scale than are the basic programs. Consequently, most rural students have access to far fewer occupational programs than urban students do. In fact, many rural students have only vocational agriculture or office occupations from which to choose.

Low population density and the attendant problem of economy of scale presents many problems for small communities. Not only are there problems of lack of financial resources, but people resources may also be found wanting. Halfvarson and O'Connor (1970), in a survey of adult music education, noted that while the interest and physical facilities were present, many small communities lacked qualified leadership. Adults wishing to continue their music education are required to go to urban centers, thus further depriving the small communities of leadership talent.

Among the causes of inferior education in rural areas cited by the National Advisory Committee on Rural Poverty (1976) was the difficulty of getting and keeping good teachers. This was especially the case for science and languages, where there was a decided absence of specialized equipment.

Small rural communities have fewer government services and smaller and less costly local governments than cities do, even on a per capita basis. Many of the public services are brought in from urban centers by outreach workers. This includes education programs for adults. The farther a rural town is from a city, the greater the difficulty in providing adequate services.

Small communities are also often characterized by nondiversified economies and limited ranges of employment opportunities. Often single-industry dominated, many small towns take on the identity of the particular industry, becoming a mill town, a mining town, a logging town, or a farming town. There are also historical rivalries between one small town and another that are kept alive through sports competitions in high schools. While such competition tends to build community identity and pride, it can also be counterproductive in situations in which cooperation is needed.

Planning in rural areas is different from planning in urban areas because of lower population, distances, smaller-scale economics, and smaller tax bases. Rogers and Whiting (1976) point out that providing needed educational and other public services demands a more consolidated effort with coordination between small communities and among many agencies. Rural values and traditions exist that are in some instances conducive and in others nonconducive to such cooperation.

Isolation

Rural communities across the country differ in the demographics of their isolation. Long distance from urban centers; physical barriers such as mountains, rivers, and weather (including winter travel restrictions); and lack of major highway systems and public transportation are the most commonly cited factors in rural isolation. There are also attitudinal factors of isolation. Rural people may be suspicious of or slow to respond to activities sponsored by outside groups. Previous experience with "hit-and-run" or "one-shot" efforts that left no residue of effect in the community and were carried out with no ongoing commitment or follow-through has understandably contributed to this sensitivity. Expectations have been raised only to have hopes dashed when there is no follow-through. This is especially the case in minority rural communities.

Lack of public transportation bars many rural people from participating in education, job training programs, social services, and even the job market. Rural America is highly dependent on the automobile and suffers acutely from such things as energy shortages and poor road conditions.

The rising cost of both cars and fuel is causing more hardship for rural inhabitants than for city dwellers. In 1980 there were only about 1,300 public buses serving nonurban areas in the entire country. The more sparsely settled states had virtually no transportation in the more rural areas. Utah had only nine bus lines, Texas had two, New Mexico had none, Idaho had three, and South Dakota had none. With the demise of rail passenger sevice to rural areas, the buses are the only remaining public links between the country and the city.

The rural family is often penalized with respect to higher education, as geographic proximity to a college campus has been found to be a major factor in determining who goes to college. Geography and access to educational opportunity are closely related.

Cultural homogeneity within the community

Anyone who has lived in more than one small town or who otherwise has had a close opportunity to observe rural communities knows that each has its own identity. Cultural identity of small towns sometimes has to do with a dominant ethnic group (e.g., Norwegians or French Basques). In many cases a particular religious or ethnic group founded and settled the town, and its influence, passed on through generations, continues to dominate. People who have not or do not fit into the dominant culture either move on or are subsumed by it.

Studies on the characteristics of the population moving from cities to smaller towns show that increased nonmetropolitan employment opportunities is the largest factor in migration and that the new migrants from the cities are selective. Dejong (1976) found that these people are younger, have higher socioeconomic status, and have smaller families than the general population of the rural areas. Inmigration trends to small towns may cause changes in the social structure, and tensions may develop between newer and older residents of communities. Rural sociologists commonly cite the phenomenon of homogeneity as the basis for stability and satisfaction among community residents. However, this will obviously be less a factor as fewer and fewer rural towns can be so characterized.

In some communities the dominant religious or ethnic group clings to values that run counter to social progress and community development. The role of women in many small towns is not changing at the pace it is in urban areas and larger communities, largely because of cultural restrictions. The National Advisory Council of Women's Educational Programs found in its 1977 investigation that rural and urban women have *not* benefited equally from the recent national concern with women's status (Clarenbuch, 1977). Groups targeted for special assistance from state and federal programs, such as displaced homemakers, are not always easily identified or willing to be singled out in the small community. People in certain leadership positions would not pursue completion of a college degree through a locally based program if it meant other people might learn that they had not already earned a degree.

Another aspect of small-town dynamics is that leadership has both formal and informal aspects. Outside groups seeking to promote local programs often are not in communication with the informal leadership and thus do not receive the necessary support to be successful. "Official" support from a cooperating agency may not be translated into the kind of legitimizing approval needed to actually make an impact. For better or worse, most issues in small towns are readily personalized, and informal networks become all the more important in the long run.

Agricultural tradition

Agriculture continues today to wield a preponderant influence over rural communities, despite the dramatic decline in the total number of farm families and the rapid growth of rural industries. As the only rural constituency in the political arena with both the cohesiveness and the power to influence policy, the farm bloc has more power at both state and federal levels than its votes would suggest. Today, while only 9 percent of the nonmetropolitan work force is in farming, agriculture production is not declining. Instead, shifts to large-scale farming have fostered growth in agriculture-related and agribusiness occupations (such as feed production, farm equipment, food processing, paper products, and marketing). The size of the labor force employed directly in production farming understates the influence of agriculture not only in politics but also in rural economics.

Although agriculture is still the *dominant influence* in many rural economies, employment in manufacturing, trade, and professional services now exceeds direct agricultural employment. Agriculture itself has changed enormously. It has become a highly sophisticated, often-specialized component of the production chain.

Agriculture and an agricultural tradition exert influence not only on politics and economics but also on values and social patterns. Rural America is still largely oriented to the family farm—if not in actual numbers, then in an agricultural tradition that perpetuates certain patterns of community mores. Rural sociologists (Mogey, 1976) tend to believe that rural communities are adapted for stability and that change tends to be disruptive and disintegrating (since it reduces boundary maintenance and religious or ethnic homogeneity). The cause-and-effect relationship to change in small towns has more direct impact due to the interdependency aspects of rural life. Industrialization of rural areas is one primary example of potentially disruptive change on the rural social system based on agrarian values. Numerous studies have documented the negative consequences of industrialization on rural social structure (e.g., Summers, 1977). The rapid rise of large agribusiness ventures and nonagricultural industry and the corresponding decline in small farms have had the effect of lowering the quality of life previously enjoyed by many communities. Shea found in a 1976 study for the Department of Agriculture that small towns surrounded by medium- to small-sized farms generally are better off in terms of community services, communication, education, civic improvement, and recreation than are towns with significant industrial development.

The agricultural tradition and adult education have been closely linked, as witnessed by the numerous program activities in small towns sponsored by the extension service, the local grange hall, etc. If the farm is the stabilizing influence on the economy, the public school is the stabilizing center of the agricultural community. Education has a very practical place in the farm community, as it serves to equip all able hands to do a better job in farming and in family life. Motivation to pursue learning is driven by real life needs and/or social expectations for involvement with other people, and in some special cases the pursuit of learning is a means of having contact with "the outside world." For agriculturally oriented rural people, the better-supported adult education programs have been those that were linked either to practical skills or to preservation of community values and enhancement of the small-town quality of life.

Participation in Adult Education

In 1940 the median years of school completed by all individuals living on rural farms was 7.6 years. In 1970 the figure rose to 9.7 years. However, during the same 30-year period, the median years of school for the counterpart population from urban areas rose from 8.6 to 12.2. One reason for the gap between urban and rural schooling is that in 1970 more than 700,000 adults in rural America had never attended school, and an additional 3 million had had less than 5 years of schooling. This pool of adults was described by Bishop (1976) as the product of an educational system that has historically "shortchanged" rural people.

The National Center for Education Statistics reports that adults are participating nationally in significantly increasing numbers in postsecondary education. According to the 1981 triennial supplement to the Current Population Survey conducted by the Bureau of the Census, over 21 million adults participated in some form of adult education: Of this total, nearly 6 million, or 28 percent, were adults living in rural areas.

Educational Needs of Rural Adults

Research data are not available that permit conclusions about comparisons of educational *needs* among rural adults versus urban dwellers. In fact, little attention has been paid in the literature to the educational needs of

FIGURE 4. Participation in Adult Education by Residential Status: 1975 and 1981

Residential status	1975		1981		Percent increase 1975–1981
	Number (in thousands)	Percent of total	Number (in thousands)	Percent of total	
Rural					
Total Population not in SMSA* (Farm and Rural Nonfarm)	46,304	31.4	52,365	31.6	13.1
Participants in Adult Education	4,364	25.6	5,865	27.6	34.4
Urban					
Total Population in SMSA*	101,098	68.6	113,464	68.4	12.2
Participants in Adult Education	12,694	74.4	15,387	72.4	21.2

From National Center for Educational Statistics, 1982.
* Standard Metropolitan Statistical Area

The data in Figure 4 indicate that only one-fourth of the enrollments are occurring in rural areas. These data also show, however, that the rate of participation in rural adult-education programs has increased by 2 percent of the population, while the urban rate of participation has decreased (also about 2 percent).

rural adults beyond the emphasis in the 1970s on attacking illiteracy. In a review of the literature on adult education in rural areas, the National Center for Research in Vocational Education concluded in an ERIC (Educational Resources Information Clearinghouse) document that

> there does not even appear to be adequate information on the nature and scope of the enterprise [adult education] in rural areas. None of the state surveys reviewed distinguished rural from urban participants or individual communities or counties. Few of the surveys took into account in any systematic way, learner-initiated individual study or informal learning networks among individuals (Bruce, 1979).

The National Advisory Council of Women's Educational Programs also found that "public statistics with specific categories for rural women are virtually non-existent." The educational needs articulated by the rural women involved in the council's investigation relate to the broadest possible range of social issues—from health care to political involvement to the preservation of rural values and regional pride.

> In spite of both geographic spread and the great diversity of culture, ethnicity, age, family circumstance, economics, and educational attainment represented by the rural women involved in the Council's investigation, there is a striking similarity of perceived need. The message brought to the Advisory Council by the rural women was essentially this: rural women want to speak for themselves and have their voices solicited and listened to; they want to be recognized as significant and contributing members of their families and of society at large; they want to have the opportunity to become independent persons, to control their own lives, to have a role in the formulation of public policy, and to share somewhat equitably in the fruits of our society (Clarenbuch, 1977).

It is increasingly the case that the differences in needs for education and public services between urban and rural citizens are dwindling and blurring in distinction. Even the smallest rural towns are affected by the dynamics of an urbanized culture, whether they are influenced by television, movies, developing new industry near them, or an increase in state and federal regulations over farms and business, schools, and towns, or the education system itself.

Sher (1977) contends that education in rural America has been motivated less by a desire to serve the indigenous needs of rural people than by an urbanizing intent. Taylor and Jones (1964) view adult education in rural areas as being in the interest of integration into society rather than of service to the interests of rural people as such. Speaking of the development of land grant colleges, they wrote:

> Their presence is inconsistent with ruralized social organization. These programs and their personnel are the connecting links which integrate the enterprises of agriculture and urbanization into a common whole, namely, the dynamic American Society.

Adding to the urbanizing influences is the phenomena of in-migration to rural areas of former city dwellers. As a result of in-migration there is a growing percentage of the rural population whose backgrounds are essentially urban to begin with. And these people bring with them needs and expectations similar to those they held as city dwellers—especially as regards furthering their education.

Swanson (1981) has written the following:

> Rural adults are not so different from city adults in their needs for lifelong learning. They are human beings with a desire to improve themselves. The vast majority of persons who live in rural America are not farmers. In fact, the economy and modern farm methods have caused many to move from the farms and learn other skills. Whether or not they remain in rural areas is dependent on whether or not these needs can be fulfilled there.

Practitioners of rural education comment that participation is steadily increasing for rural adult programs and that student expectations are also broadening. As Margery Walker, with the Rural Education program at the University of Alaska, has written (1981):

> Rural residents now want more than occasional courses sanctioned for field delivery by campus departments. They seek coherent programs in their communities which will result in a tangible body of skills and knowledge, and in degrees and certification competitive to those of their campus counterparts. Rural students are extremely diverse in their interests, heritages, educational levels, life styles and economic situation, but they share a common difficulty in securing access to college and university programs suited to their current needs.

One of the primary needs resulting from rural isolation is meaningful interaction with one's peers. Practitioners of rural education generally agree that social interaction is a primary motivator of adults to pursue education programs in rural communities. Much adult education in small towns is also centered around social benefits to the community—such as parenting classes; practical skills for farm, home, or small business; health; nutrition; local history; culture and arts; etc. Because the lives of most rural residents are not sharply divided between relationships at home, work, church, and school, adult education is an extension of the several roles and functions of people in the small community into yet another common social activity.

Education serves as an antidote to severe isolation. It is a means of linking nearby communities with one another and also a primary vehicle for bringing the outside world to the rural community. The presence of a visiting professor of philosophy, politics, or literature, for example, is a social, as well as an educational, event in a small town.

Other social needs met by education are the reduction of illiteracy and poverty, the provision of outward mobility for those feeling trapped in a small-town environment, and the development of leadership that can function effectively in an increasingly complex society.

Some social patterns and values may mitigate against the value of education for adults. Conservative political views, independence and regionalism, a male-oriented politic, attitudes of frustration in the face of scarce resources, and a general lack of placing value in learning beyond the youth school years can work against education programs for adults if not recognized and dealt with as part of the social fabric of many communities.

Having recognized such potential detracting forces, it must be stated that rural people come from a heritage of resourcefulness, cooperation, and pride in community. As the University for Man in Kansas has found, people-to-people learning is a powerful potential force in small towns. Each person has some skill or knowledge to share with someone else, and the perception of needs as well as educational-program delivery should definitely recognize this potential force.

Despite the lack of systematic surveys and national data on educational needs for rural adults, one can conclude from what has been written by practitioners that the following are generally evidenced in most small communities:

1. Rural people are looking for education that relates more immediately to their needs and has a practical consequence.

2. Rural people want to have a role in planning and directing the post-secondary education programs offered in their communities.

3. Rural residents want coherent programs of study, not just bits and pieces. On-campus residency requirements are an example of university policy that runs counter to rural needs.

4. Rural poverty is more prevalent than in urban areas, and the people are much more geographically dispersed. Rural people need job training near their homes, which probably entails individualization of training programs.

5. Rural isolation effects people in different ways. However, it can generally be said that the usual emphasis on content in education must be augmented with critical thinking skills and the stimulation of intellectual curiosity.

6. Rural women need educational programs that are offered to women only. This is particularly true in subject areas that are male-dominated, such as mathematics and science and technical/industrial areas. There is evidence that learning is enhanced in sex-segregated groups for rural women.

7. There is also a need for coeducational learning, family-centered programs, and intergenerational programs for rural communities to undergird basic rural values of family life and community pride and involvement.

8. Rural residents need education and training that empower them to be agents of change in their communities—to become empowered to effect economic and social decisions that will determine the future quality of life.

9. Rural residents need educational support services appropriate to their education, ethnic background, and level of skills and resources for balancing job, family, and community responsibilities.

Types of Rural Education Programs

The noted journalist Richard Margolis (founding chairman of Rural America, Inc.) has written the following:

> It seems hard to escape the conclusion that something significant is occurring in rural America, something that rural people need to understand. Education, both formal and informal, can provide a framework for the pursuit of that understanding. (1981)

Whether rural postsecondary educational programs are serving to integrate the new in-migrants into rural towns, or to empower the local residents to resist the disfiguration of their land by outside industrial interests, or to enhance the capacity for an individual to realize his or her personal aspirations through learning, there is a massive effort across the nation. Libraries, community colleges, community-based volunteer organizations, state and federal agencies, colleges and universities, business and industries, churches, and cooperative extension units are participating in the effort to make lifelong learning opportunity a reality for rural people.

For the most part, individuals and organizations offering educational programs for rural communities are isolated from one another and do not benefit from a high level of exchange of working strategies, results, etc. The purpose of this chapter is, first, to give recognition to a number of outstanding projects and programs that are having success in overcoming some of the problems addressed by rural areas. Second, by summarizing types of programs and citing a few examples of effective approaches in each category, it is hoped that readers will gain useful ideas from this exchange and will also feel free to contact any of the programs referred to if they desire to follow up with specific inquiries.

The past few years have witnessed much experimentation and effort using new delivery systems from colleges and universities to reach off-campus adults. Recent efforts to form consortia in sponsoring credit televised courses or to combine resources to offer joint degree programs are encouraging signs that institutions are not only experimenting but that some are moving to break down institutional and largely artificial "turfs," which tend to divert resources and energy and seem to have little long-term impact on any "competing" institution. Rural residents prefer, according to recent surveys, the type of learning situation represented by an instructor in a group setting. However, appreciating the access afforded by television, computer-assisted instruction, and other means of "remote delivery," rural people are adapting to these new methodologies and are participating in increasing numbers in college degree programs with these features. Schools that combine media with teleconferencing, site visits by faculty, group discussion, local mentors, and other support strategies seem to be more responsive to learner needs than those that simply send out programs for the individual to get through on his or her own, without aides.

Aside from programs that simply blanket a large geographical area (correspondence study or public broadcast courses), most colleges that have sought to serve rural communities distant from their campuses have done so through some form of local community center or contact agency. Use of local organizers, mentors, or managers by the outreach efforts appears to be an important strategy for effective programming.

Clearly, the focus of this publication is on colleges and universities that seek to serve rural adults. However, there are many other agencies involved in the total enterprise of rural postsecondary education. Without attempting to be comprehensive, several noncollege-based providers are cited as examples. It is hoped that postsecondary institutions can not only learn from what other agencies are doing but also recognize the value of those contributions, and find ways to actively collaborate in resource sharing.

GED and ABE Programs

The federal government invested a considerable effort in supporting the development of Adult Basic Education (ABE) programs during the 1960s and 1970s. One of the better-documented programs was a 13-state effort headquartered at Morehead State University in Kentucky. Rurally isolated people in the mountain areas of Appalachia were the target audience. Another program was the Communi-Link Project of Colorado State University. These programs generated a number of innovative approaches, including audio-cassette learning packages, paraprofessionals as teaching assistants, and newspaper instruction.

In most areas of the country ABE programs and the General Education Diploma (GED) are sponsored by school districts and community colleges, with federal funding assistance. Research studies show that the best results are obtained when attention is given to diagnosis, counseling, and the teaching of basic skills in conjunction with employment and community natural settings.

Occupational Training

In conjunction with a federal focus on literacy in the 1960s there were the beginnings of what is now a major emphasis on job training to overcome poverty in rural areas. Under the Comprehensive Employment and Training Act (CETA), training programs have sprung up across the country. However, there has not been much published in the literature about their effectiveness. A notable exception is reported in the Rural Jobs from Rural Public Worker Survey, conducted in 1978 by the National Rural Center. This project addressed the condition of labor market referral, affirmative action, and job training activities on federal construction sites in rural areas of the South. One of the more innovative approaches was the Mountain Plains Education and Economic Development Program, which enrolled whole families in a residential program for training. There were family management skills de-velopment programs as well as job placement counseling services provided for the family as a unit. However, it was determined that working with people outside their unchanged back-at-home environment was too artifi-cial an approach, and little success was reported.

For the most part, government-sponsored job-training programs involve short-term (up to one year), intensive, on-the-job training, coupled with basic-skills instruction provided by a local agency or college. There are a few examples of remote delivery technology, as in the case of the Singer Corporation materials for career development, which are being used in rural areas. The lack of employment opportunities in many rural areas precludes a comprehensive emphasis for on-the-job training. Many CETA trainees have had to leave their local towns to go to urban areas for training and employment.

There are more than 1,000 small, rural community colleges and voca-tional training centers providing campus-based job training. These institu-tions work closely with local employers, as well as with CETA and other agencies, in developing cooperative programs. However, these efforts are both fragmented and not well financed. In fiscal year 1978 rural counties in the United States spent $14.8 per capita on vocational adult education, whereas metropolitan counties spent $44.8 per capita.

In 1980 the U.S. Department of Education, Office of Vocational and Adult Education (OVAE), published the booklet *Rural Education Programs That Work*. Thirty-two states shared exemplary projects in adult community and vocational education through this publication. Names and addresses of contact programs are also mentioned.

Another major aspect of vocational education for rural areas is continuing education for a large number of occupational and professional groups. A study of the needs for occupational recertification in Minnesota (Minnesota Research Coordinating Unit, 1982) found that 44 out of 78 occupations reviewed had a state-mandated continuing education requirement. The majority of states report problems in providing access to such update training for rural residents.

Counseling and Information Programs

Through the Educational Information Centers Program, the federal government provided funds that led to the establishment of a number of outreach centers in rural areas. Two projects that the Fund for the Improvement of Postsecondary Education sponsored contained elements of what the majority of programs attempt to do.

Outreach Adult Counseling and Information Services (OACIS) was established by Colorado Mountain Community College (CMCC) in 1977. The college's district serves a five-county, 5,700-square-mile area. Characteristics of this mountainous district include difficult travel, adverse weather conditions, and a diverse population ranging from resort towns to mining and ranching communities. To address these characteristics, CMCC operates eight fully staffed community-based instructional centers. Using outreach educational counselors, the college assists individuals in goal setting, evaluating options, decision making, and contacting appropriate resources. Although based in the community centers, the counselors also reach people through libraries, on work sites, and at places of residence.

Project ACCESS (Career Information and Advisement Center) is administered by the Center for Education Manpower Resources, a community-based, private, nonprofit agency located in Ukiah, California. Counselors from ACCESS work with individuals and small groups to help adults define their interests within the realities of the rural area, including geographic isolation, limited population and varieties of jobs, and limited training opportunities. ACCESS offers advice and information services to supplement and enhance institutional programs of the area. It also serves as a library for agencies providing up-to-date information about educational programs and local labor market conditions. An interesting feature of the program is its emphasis on word-of-mouth information rather than on printed matter. The counselors believe this is more in keeping with how other information is disseminated in small communities, and they also want to be able to serve people of limited reading ability.

Libraries play a key role in disseminating educational materials and providing information in all communities. The North Central Regional Library System is a cooperative network of 81 public libraries in 13 counties in Iowa. A variety of continuing-educational experiences are available through the library network. For example, the North Central Regional Library provides culture kits from the Office of International Education at the state university. The kits are multimedia armchair travel experiences and are heavily used by senior citizen programmers. Most of the librarians also serve as information and referral agents. They utilize materials from the Area Agency on Aging as well as from the area extension office and the community colleges. They help refer adults to other agencies for training and also help bring classes from those agencies into their communities. The Northwest Iowa Regional Library in Sioux City, Iowa, has taken its services a step further in attempting to create a network by publishing the Rural Library Service Newsletter, which describes successful projects for adult learners.

Economic Development

In addition to traditional vocational training programs for adults, a number of initiatives aimed at helping rural communities improve their economic resources and general welfare have been fostered by colleges and universities as well as by newly organized, private, nonprofit organizations.

The Federation of Southern Cooperatives at Epes, Alabama, is establishing a noncollegiate, occupational institution for rural community economic development. Kentucky Highlands Investment Corporation (KHIC) is also a private, nonprofit development company. It has pioneered the tactic of using entrepreneurial talent to meet the economic development goals of a region. KHIC offers rural people access to investment capital (through a loan fund) and provides them with highly focused technical assistance. Local businesses, education agencies, and social agencies assist in identifying prospective entrepreneurs and help with some of the technical assistance.

Tuskegee Institute in Alabama operates a Human Resources Development Center, which coordinates community-based efforts in 30 counties. These programs fall into several broad areas, including agriculture and resource development, community education, youth services, business development, manpower training, community food and nutrition programs, and international programs.

Seven colleges and universities in western Colorado joined to form the Western Colorado Rural Communities Program. This project has had two major objectives: (1) the development of the individual institution's capability and capacity to engage in rural community development programming, and (2) the development of an interinstitutional framework for supporting individual institutional community development efforts.

Community-based educational programs to assist rural people with concerns related to economic development have sprung up in many parts of the country, some supported by foundations such as the W.K. Kellogg Foundation and others supported by state legislatures. In Oregon, the legislature allocated monies to two regional colleges—Southern Oregon State College and Eastern Oregon State College—for the purpose of enabling these institutions to become responsive to the needs of rural communities for economic development and for education and training programs. Similar programs have been launched in Alaska and Minnesota. The Countryside Council Program in southwestern Minnesota emphasizes local citizen involvement and control over programs provided by a consortium of area colleges. Sixty-seven local citizens representing nineteen counties and nine colleges meet monthly to consider priority issues affecting the quality of life in their rural communities. The practical tradition of "work" bees, in which people joined forces to harvest grain or to build a schoolhouse in the past, are being revived by the council's approach to problem solving.

Adult Education

Another very important initiative of the 1970s for rural communities was the group of adult education programs of a volunteer nature. In the province of Alberta, Canada, Local Further Education Councils have been established to mobilize all available resources to offer coordinated, comprehensive continuing education courses to adults. These councils are composed of community volunteers, as individuals and as representatives of organizations, who offer courses in the community. The University for Man in Kansas has been a very successful program for developing community-based volunteer adult learning programs. Based on the free university model, the community learning centers connect people who want to teach or learn with the resources to meet their needs. Over 200 sponsored and independent free universities have sprung up nationally. The University of Man is now organized in 35 small towns in Kansas and serves more than 30,000 participants. Leaders are volunteers, and courses are held in churches, libraries, parks, school classrooms, and people's homes. Most free universities are noncollegiate credit in nature. A few have also served as vehicles for credit programs, such as the coastal learning cooperatives developed by the University of Maine at Augusta.

Special Rural Populations

Rural life in America has changed dramatically in recent years, and issues concerning the roles of women are being addressed by some rural programs. Rural women need educational opportunities that are based on acceptance of the fundamental values of rural life but that prepare rural women to deal with changes. Washington State University, the University of Idaho, and Lewis and Clark State College have developed a women's educational outreach program that sponsors community-based workshops, led by local facilitators, to teach rural women needed skills and insights for changing roles.

Florida International University has a program whose target is the learning needs of farm workers in rural communities. Through community education circles, basic literacy groups, life-planning and support groups, language immersions, and training in skills using mobile vans, this university is serving more than 8,000 adults in their local communities.

The University of Alaska's Rural Education Program is working with native villages to upgrade leadership and business skills, to develop an effective delivery system of continuing education in the state, and to involve rural people in their villages in the development of needed adult programs.

Campus-Based Programs Focusing on Rural Needs

A number of programs have been initiated by colleges and universities in recent years that address some of the special needs for training of people serving rural communities. In the fields of health care, education, law, and social work, there are now institutions that specialize in preparing professionals for understanding rural communities.

Social worker training at the University of Montana, Missoula, and Eastern Washington State University focuses on rural settings and small communities. Practitioners of social casework in small communities must be generalists rather than specialists; they must understand and relate to natural helping networks and to the traditions and mores of small communities. By offering special courses and seminars on rural sociology, small-town politics, casework practices for rural areas, and field experience in the small communities, these programs are assisting new professionals to adapt better to and be of more service to the communities.

At the University of Montana the training of lawyers is also taking a specifically rural focus. Traditional legal education has been reviewed, particularly as it relates in methods and assumptions to the needs of lawyers practicing alone or with a few others in a rural setting.

Migrant and seasonal farm workers have restricted access to health services in many rural areas because of cultural and language barriers. The University of Washington MEDEX (Medical Extern) program trains Hispanic adults to serve as community health advocates by developing their skills in counseling, health education, and medical screening. The content of the training is designed for bilingual students and covers the specific health needs of the migrant farm worker.

Vanderbilt University's Center for Health Services has established programs to relate social, economic, and political structures of rural health and health services to training health professionals. Nursing, medical, and physician's-assistant students visit rural communities and have supervised clinical experience in these communities. They also have orientation programs dealing with health care issues in Appalachia and their relationships to the history, politics, and socioeconomic structures of the region. Students are also encouraged to help in community projects or to start new ones, such as nutrition education programs.

At Washington State University, the W. K. Kellogg Foundation funded a program called the Partnership for Rural Improvement that concentrates on leadership development for small rural towns, providing training and resources for elected and appointed officials and volunteer groups.

At Eastern Oregon State College, elementary and secondary school teachers are trained to serve migrant farm worker communities through a bilingual degree program. Students in the program spend part of their second college year and the entire fourth year working on-site in Hispanic community classrooms. They also take special courses in Chicano culture and traditions.

In South Dakota, Sinte Gleska College is educating adults who can serve in Rosebud Indian Reservation schools and help preserve Lakota tribal arts, traditions, and practices. Sinte Gleska College is a tribally controlled Indian community college offering six associate of arts and two bachelor of science programs.

In Alaska, Project X-CED (Cross-Cultural Education) trains native Alaskans to become teachers in their own village schools. The University of Alaska at Fairbanks provides faculty who live in the local communities and offer the local teacher educational training through multimedia courses produced by the university. The project also employs wide use of teleconferencing instruction.

Industry-Based Training

The Western Virginia Institute of Technology is an example of a rural-based institution that has developed outreach programs with cooperating employers to provide adults with training on the employer's site. Using a combination of group and individualized techniques developed in 5 years of labor-related education, the Southern Appalachian Labor School is offering education on the work site to 300 workers per semester. Coal miners, chemical workers, railway personnel—the industrial work force of the area—gather in union halls and community meeting places to work toward their baccalaureate degrees.

Most rural community colleges utilize cooperative education programs and other approaches to provide training in conjunction with employment in local business and industry. One example is Southwest Community College in Cumberland, Kentucky, which offers programs such as mining technology, reclamation technology, and medical laboratory technology in cooperation with local industry. The college's full-time enrollment is 382. The approach is especially practical for small colleges that cannot afford extensive training facilities. Industries themselves are accelerating inhouse training programs in the face of technological change. New technology is squeezing the unskilled worker out of the labor market and putting a premium on ever more advanced training. Technical employment rose at more than twice the rate of other types of employment in rural areas during the 1970s. Thousands of displaced workers must adjust to other industries and occupations to earn their livelihood.

Industry-based training has turned in recent years to new educational technologies, such as interactive video- and computer-assisted instruction to upgrade programs and increase cost efficiencies. Weyerhauser Corporation in Tacoma, Washington, uses interactive video programs, which the company believes are more effective than instructor-oriented, lecture-type programs because the student is forced to listen carefully and respond correctly before advancing. However, these technologies are expensive, and only a few rural-based firms have utilized them at this time.

New Delivery Systems

In describing the different types of programs offered in rural adult education, mention was made in some cases of the use of new forms of communications technology to reach isolated learners. Another way to provide a typology of rural programs is to describe them according to the particular remote delivery system they are utilizing. A recent publication entitled *Meeting Learners' Needs through Telecommunications*, by the American

Association of Higher Education (AAHE), provides an overview of current models in postsecondary education. This survey is only a brief review of some model programs.

Telephone instruction

Use of telephones for instruction (and class discussion) is taking place in a number of states and localities. The University of Wisconsin operates a statewide network, as do the states of Alaska, Washington, and New Mexico. Eastern Montana College sponsors telephone courses in one totally rural section of Montana. These networks feature teleconferencing speakers and microphones at established centers. Students meet in small groups at the centers and receive "live" instruction from a campus-based instructor. Signal devices allow students to ask questions and to enter into two-way discussion. All students at the centers can hear all other students as well as the instructor. Up to 30 locations are served simultaneously by the teleconferencing system. Some instructors supplement phone instruction with printed materials, slide-and-tape presentations, and transparencies or prepared videotapes.

The advantage of the Eastern Montana College program is that all 30 sites are in small rural communities, whereas in the case of the state of Washington, only 3 of the 30 sites are in rural communities. As a result, many people in the eastern half of Washington still must drive as far as 100 miles to reach one of the centers. Statewide telephone networks are reaching place-bound adults effectively; however, the politics of population density (as well as economics) is precluding emphasis on small, rural communities at this time.

Television instruction

There are three basic types of outreach to rural areas through television technology: (1) commercially produced courses developed by colleges, (2) videotaped regular campus courses, and (3) live interactive televised instruction. Most rural-based small colleges do not have the resources to purchase commercially produced television courses. However, recent marketing of these courses through consortia utilizing public television has made possible cost-effective participation. Many colleges are receiving these courses through cable television to their campus communities; some are offering them through outreach centers that utilize videotapes provided by the consortium and copied on-campus for local distribution.

Foothill College in California is utilizing public broadcasting courses as well as campus courses in a broad effort with 30 other colleges to utilize public media for instruction and information. Foothill established a toll-free telephone information system to help adults get information on the courses and degree programs. The Appalachian Educational Satellite Program is an interstate program that uses public television to offer college-credit courses with a degree program emphasis. Institutions as far away as the University of Idaho access the programs with satellite receiver dishes.

Another format for televised instruction is the so-called instant-replay approach, in which regular campus courses are videotaped and then distributed the next day to off-campus viewing locations. Stanford University and Colorado State Universities pioneered this type of outreach to industry for engineering degrees. Western Oregon State College has been sending videotapes to school districts for teacher training and has been cooperating with Eastern Oregon State College, which both uses the former's tapes in its region and makes tapes of liberal arts courses to send to centers in support of its external degree program in general studies. The videotapes are often accompanied by other materials. Sometimes an instructor is available through prearranged conference telephone calls, and in many cases the instructors make a visit to each of the centers during the term their particular course is being offered.

The role of local, rural college participation in video instruction is most often that of broker, which means offering the academic credit to its constituents, providing information and advising, and sometimes offering supplemental activities such as local discussion groups, teleconferencing, etc.

Kirkwood Community College in Cedar Rapids, Iowa, which serves a seven-county rural area, is developing courses for delivery on a microwave, two-way audio and visual system. With a focus on laboratory courses (rather than traditional lecture-and-discussion courses), the college is pioneering fully interactive remote instruction at eight locations in southeastern Iowa. The University of Idaho sends videotapes to and from satellite links and is also utilizing microwave relays to teach courses live from campus to Washington State University as well as to several industry sites. The opportunity for students to see and hear the instructor and vice versa, once it becomes cost-effective, will be the next major step in serving rural communities according to many telecommunications experts.

Certain courses at Cuyahoga Community College in Ohio are broadcast live by special telephone equipment and color television to hospitalized and home-bound handicapped adults. This system also permits delayed television replay. Because of the telephone component, students are able to participate in class discussions and to benefit more directly from on-campus proceedings. Three hospitals, thus far, have participated in the hookup, which includes audio-video microwave and cable television.

Radio and newspaper instruction

Although much attention has been focused on television, particularly interactive approaches, radio and newspapers remain the lowest-cost and most readily accessible public media to serve the rural adult. The major limitation at this time has been that such courses have been those of a general adult education interest and have not been developed to serve the adult pursuing a degree program. National Public Radio has recently announced its intention, through participation on a grant program of the Annenberg School of Communications, to work with colleges developing degree-oriented radio courses.

Independent and Individualized Study Programs

Most major universities offer correspondence and independent study courses that can be used toward college degrees (although many place severe limitations on the number of such courses that can be applied to a degree program). Across the country, participation in correspondence study is on the decline. This may be partially explained by the dramatic increase in television courses and by the development of off-campus instructional programs.

An important project for rural outreach is that of Central Technical Community College in Columbus, Nebrasksa, which is using individualized instruction technology on-campus as well as in off-campus centers. By forming cooperative arrangements with organizations in a number of small communities, the college was able to establish remote learning centers without costly duplication of facilities. At each center a resident coordinator acts as mentor for the individualized packaged courses sent to the center from the campus. The local community coordinator supervises students, maintains learning center equipment, administers tests, and provides counseling and information. Campus faculty correct tests, answer questions, and provide directions to their course students by telephone and written communications. During the first 2 years, 90 percent of the students surveyed said they had received more than they expected from the courses taken through this program.

Integrated Systems Approaches

A program currently under way in western Minnesota that is bringing together many of the types of programs listed in this chapter is Project ENLIST (Educational Network Linking Institutions, Students, and Technology). ENLIST is a project that is developing stronger linkages among 15 postsecondary education institutions (community colleges, universities, and technical institutes), community education programs, libraries, and telecommunication providers. It has created an ongoing cooperative advising and assessment service for rural adult learners and delivers those services by utilizing existing telecommunications technology. A somewhat similar comprehensive network has been developed by Eastern Oregon State College. These two national demonstration projects, funded by the Fund for the Improvement of Postsecondary Education and their sponsoring institutions, will perhaps serve as models for integrating all learning resources for adults in a rural area through the building of working partnerships among all education providers.

Program
Development
and Strategies

> Education is no longer seen as the monopoly of educational institutions and their teachers. We now perceive that resources for learning are everywhere in our environment and that people can get help in their learning from a variety of other people. The modern task of education, therefore, becomes one of finding new ways to link learners with learning resources.

Malcolm Knowles's (1980) definition of education's modern task is a very appropriate one, especially for rural communities. Some linkages are firmly in place, having existed for many generations: the tie in small towns between the public school and the family; the tie in farming communities between the agriculturalists and the county extension program; the tie between Sunday schools, churches, and rural family life. There are a number of important linkages however, that are not so firmly in place: the tie between colleges and universities and the continuing education of professionals serving in rural areas; the tie between recent developments in communications technology and providing access to postsecondary learning in small towns; the tie(s) between local rural schools and other education providers within a region or state and providing cooperative programs and (again) access to adult education; the tie between the economic development of rural towns and educational opportunities for workers and the community at large; and the tie between the slower-paced, small, rural community and the faster-paced, rapidly changing world beyond of politics, technology, and social and cultural transitions.

Adult educators working in rural areas face some particularly difficult barriers in making effective linkages or otherwise providing postsecondary learning opportunities. Many of these barriers are inherent in the characteristics of the rural community that were discussed in the preceding section: geographical isolation, lack of population density, small economies of scale, lack of public transportation and other services, and traditions and mores that may run counter to postsecondary educational values. Effective educational program development requires new strategies, some of which are reviewed in the following discussion.

Gaining Access to People in Their Communities

The first task for the rural adult educator is that of gaining access to his or her clientele. On the surface this may not appear to be a difficult task. Especially in a town of less than 2,500 residents, one might assume there is a "captive audience" for adult education. In actual practice the gaining of access to prospective learners can be a difficult and even complex process. For example, a college that seeks to establish outreach centers in rural towns will have several options as to location, type of facility, and local sponsor. Some institutions rely on a single agency, such as county cooperative extension offices, to act as the outreach location for their programs across a given state or region. The advantage of this is that county extension units have a clientele with whom they are already in contact, as well as a communication system. The disadvantages include the fact that in some counties the extension program may not have as solid an image as in others or that its constituents may not represent the primary groups the program is seeking to serve. By conducting an informal survey, it can be determined which of the several possible local sponsors would be the most helpful and locally credible and would provide the maximum point of access to potential students.

While spending one or two days in a small town, a person can observe walk-in usage of an agency, can ask people where they go for information or whom they would contact about educational opportunities, etc. It has been a practice of some architects who design public facilities to request that the building be opened and used for a week or two before the sidewalks are poured. The concrete is then placed in the already-established walking paths. Adult educators can follow this same principle if they will seek first to understand each community's already-established paths of communication. In addition to factors of usage and location, the personnel of the agencies are themselves critical determinants since they can have either a positive or a negative attitude toward the presence of outside groups providing programs in their community. This is particularly the case when they think certain turf issues are at stake and if they perceive the college as competitive with their own programs.

When Eastern Oregon State College established its program to serve a 10-county rural area, it found that no single agency was equally well positioned to serve as a key communicator in all locations where they sought to provide contact centers. In order to gain maximum impact in each location, they selected the most favorable cosponsor, which led to utilizing a county library in one area, a chamber of commerce in another, a leased office building, an extension office, etc.

When Bloomsburg State College in Pennsylvania found that it was not being successful in small communities because of a lack of acceptance as an outside institution, it affiliated itself with a network of local women's groups. Under the cosponsorship of these local groups the program immediately began to draw people who previously had not come forward.

Not only are the concepts of established communications patterns and local credibility important in establishing centers, they are also obviously indispensible to program effectiveness in publicizing , promoting, and developing programs utilizing these local channels. Every community has certain places most people go at least once a week, where they read announcements (if well placed). In most rural towns the radio is the number-one means of communication. The weekly newspapers in small towns are also read cover to cover. A recent meeting of a continuing education association included a session on marketing programs for rural areas. An individual from a large urban university was asking the group for suggestions on how to reach the rural areas of his state with extension classes. The first answer he got seemed to puzzle him, but it drew nods of agreement from most of the practitioners in the room. The answer was simple: "Advertise in the church bulletins!"

No program goes forward without people first hearing about it and forming a judgment that it is a good thing. Paths that people will travel to adult learning programs are already established in rural towns, and practitioners need to build their sidewalks within those paths whenever possible.

Developing Local Involvement

As mentioned above, the first step in gaining local involvement is the utilization of local channels of communication that are already functioning. The second principle is closely related to the first: the establishment of local advisory groups. Some programs form their groups largely as a representative council made up of all organizations in the community with a specific interest or role in adult education. The other model for advisory groups is a steering committee primarily made up of consumers of the programs and of advocates for programs, who may or may not represent community agencies. There are, of course, combinations of these two models, and, indeed, a combination approach seems to have the most merit. For strong program development it is essential to be certain that all groups are aware of your program, understand it in relation to the community's needs, and understand their particular agency role as well. It is also very important to have a group that is knowledgeable about all programs in the community in order to coordinate and schedule efforts. Also, resource sharing is facilitated by a representative council. On the other hand, representatives or heads of local agencies tend to be very busy themselves and are rightfully preoccupied with their own programs. As a result, a steering group comprised of participants or advocates is usually needed to supplement the representative group in the day-to-day activities.

In the majority of small towns there are one or more key political figures who can play a major role for good or ill in the success of outreach programming. By "political," we mean influential leadership that may be formally designated or informally active in providing the sanctions and approvals for "what really works in this town." In one small town there is a retired judge who still maintains an "office" above the post office. Although he may go to that office no more than once a month just to be seen there, he is still consulted every morning at the local coffee shop on any matter of perceived importance in that town. In another small town those people who decide most of the long-range agenda for their area are informally invited to be at a particular lake for the opening day of fishing. To get invited is a major political task for a newcomer. If a person does not get invited and wants to have input, that person needs to get his or her views to someone who will be there that day.

For elected and appointed officials, colleges and universities often actually have supplemental or public resources to offer to these people so that seeking their endorsement is not just a one-way street. These mutual alliances can be real dividends for a high level of local involvement.

Probably the most powerful form of building local involvement in programs occurs when the purposes of the educational institution and a second group in the community can be successfully merged into one program event. Continuing education programs have traditionally utilized industry training programs and professional organizations to broker academic credit. In a small community, this concept is applied in several ways.

1. A local historical society can develop a public lecture series that the college offers for optional credit. In one case we are familiar with, the local museum curator was advised by a college professor on how to develop a

lecture series. The program was set up for multiple levels of participation ranging from noncredit to high school, community college, four-year, and even graduate credit (for local teachers preparing materials for their classes). The college and the local resource person collaborated on roles and responsibilities for instruction to maximize involvement. In this town of 2,300 people, 90 took the history class.

2. Colleges can assist public agencies (hospitals, schools, social agencies) in applying for and receiving state and federal grant monies for training programs that they cosponsor. Often small community agencies do not have personnel who are adequately trained to prepare competitive grant applications. It has been demonstrated across the nation that rural areas (as contrasted to large school systems) get fewer federal dollars for educational grant programs because of a lack of grant-writing expertise and resources.

3. Colleges and universities can cooperate with local high schools, community colleges, CETA, etc., in jointly offering programs. They can also, even though on a smaller scale, work closely with local industry and businesses in employee development programs.

Determing Needs and Relating Needs to Institutional Mission

The question of needs assessments for adults in rural areas is a perplexing one given the typical situation of a dispersed population that does not have concentrations of people in any one location or centering on common learning needs. The fact that, for the most part, rural people have the same needs as their urban counterparts results in a list of needs that is long; and therefore there are obvious problems in developing needs assessments. One does not want to open the door for a wide range of input on needs, only to have to deny most of them due to lack of resources or sufficient numbers of people with common needs. In a town of 1,900 people the local paper sent out a survey and received requests for more than 300 separate adult education classes. Only 7 of the topics listed, however, had more than 10 people expressing the same interest. The college that responded to the newspaper's attempt to promote a program was able to hold only two of the classes needed because of a requirement that it had to enroll 12 people to finance the course. In other words, 298 of the expressed needs were not served; thus raising expectations only to have them dashed for lack of response capability. Often, rural people do not have a sufficient understanding of the role and scope of postsecondary education to be in a position to express their needs adequately. They are aware of their towns' problems—unemployment, welfare, water quality, and lack of public services generally—but they often cannot express their needs in terms of adult education.

This is partly due to unawareness of the possibilities or options and partly to a difficulty in communications with institutions (which have a vocabulary all their own and perhaps an aloof posture; as perceived by the average citizen). We hear a familiar circular dialogue that goes like this: "What do you want?" "Well, what do you offer?"

The issue of needs assessments begins largely as a question of institutional mission. If a college's or university's primary mission is to provide access to degree programs or professional/occupational credentials, then needs assessments do not address curriculum as much as they do delivery systems and support services. On the other hand, community-based programs may already have a local delivery system in place but may not be certain of what people want as far as subject areas are concerned. Most outreach programs also assess preferred modes of instruction, location, time-of-day preferences, etc., of their targeted service groups.

A few principles of needs assessments can serve as a basic guideline, although specific situations will offer some exceptions and also some unique issues.

1. Public surveys in rural communities raise general expectations. Even if the sample size is not great, word-of-mouth communication will inform the majority of community members of the survey and its items. As a result, survey aims should be modest, the number of issues limited, the results published openly, and follow-up provided, even if the results are not largely positive.

2. A community-needs conference is a good mechanism for prioritization of a long list of needs. This one-day session brings together all interested individuals and groups in a workshop. Here they form teams to address needs in subject areas; then, as a group, they develop a list of priorities for the coming year. Strategies for matching local and out-of-area resources to needs can also be pursued during this working community conference.

3. *Targeting* groups, as is done by marketing specialists, is a useful tool for rural areas as well as for cities. Mothers of preschool children, adults facing retirement, community-elected leaders, secretaries, and small business managers all represent target populations with specific educational needs, patterns of employment, availability for classes, etc. For programs serving more than one community, needs-assessment methodologies developed in one town for its target groups will generally also be applicable without modification to other towns in the region. Targeting tends to produce better enrollments than "shotgun" or "you-all come" approaches.

4. Needs assessments should generally be conducted within the parameters of the available resources for educational delivery. Many educators have had the experience of receiving high responses to a suggested class only to find a mere three people in attendance the first night. Something went wrong with the matching of interest in subject to delivery or access.

A part of the delivery-system issue and the targeting issue is the definition of workable service parameters for a given area. A college in South Dakota determined that drawing circles with a 50 mile-radius around key communities would provide the most useful definition of target service areas for its region. The college then proceeded to establish its outreach centers with this kind of configuration in mind. Community colleges in Nebraska have their main campuses along the interstate highway that divides the state in the middle. Population centers tend to be located along the interstate highway, and it has been logical in this situation to develop outreach branches off this main trunk of commerce and communication. In regions with many mountains, rivers, or other geographical features that separate communities (such as Alaska and Oregon), geography is the primary determinant of service-delivery configurations. The particular service configuration determines whose needs are assessed, at what point in time, and with reference to what available programs.

5. Needs assessments should be conducted on an interagency basis whenever possible, with institutional mission clearly focused and items clearly stated and realistically served if prioritized. In small towns assessments need not be highly formalized. Although it can be conducted in a variety of ways, oral communication is preferred to written methods.

Fostering Interinstitutional Collaboration

While duplication of services and competition between educational institutions are generally problems (especially for tax-supported programs), nowhere is duplication more difficult to justify than in the rural areas, where it is truly wasteful and clearly irresponsible. With educational resources already scarce and in some cases nonexistent, no community can afford any duplication of programs. Wherever there is duplication, there are other needs going unmet as a result of the wasted efforts. Where there is overt competition, often neither program can survive, and, of course, the community is the loser.

Practitioners of adult education in rural areas will confront problems of resource management or competition at various levels. There are programs offered statewide or even nationally that make no attempt whatsoever to coordinate with local programming efforts. There are "circuit-rider" programs that come into town for a weekend workshop and then leave, never to be seen again. These are often programmed from a long distance with a single local sponsor or no sponsor (e.g., the familiar workshops at chain-ownership motels, etc.). There are many programs, both local and outside the community, that perceive their programs as so unique that they require no coordination. Church groups often view themselves in this manner, as do, sometimes, extension programs, the YMCA, and the YWCA. Actually, no program in a small community exists to serve adults in a vacuum, because all programs compete for the available discretionary time of the adult. Often these adults drive long distances and make considerable financial commitments for child care, etc., to participate.

Most locally based, rural adult programs have established advisory councils or coordination committees for joint schedule planning and program coordination. These groups also assist with location of facilities and other local resources and advise sponsoring institutions on policies and programs for their area.

Memorandums of agreement between educational institutions such as secondary schools, community colleges, colleges, and universities that are serving a common area of a region are very useful. They assist the practitioners by providing guidelines for cooperation and protocol for communications and effective problem solving. Some agreements also can reduce the specter of competition if they address appropriate roles and responsibilities of all parties to the agreement. Formal agreements for facilities usage also make possible the kind of economies needed for efficient program operation in small communities.

Institutions outside the area that are offering outreach programs will need information from the local staff and local institutions about the kinds of resources they have available, that can be obtained reasonably and readily, and those that are not attainable. More will be discussed with reference to institutional resource management in Chapter 4, "Issues for Postsecondary Institutions."

Some other mechanisms of institutional collaboration that have been successful in rural areas include the following.

1. Joint hiring of instructional staff between two institutions (secondary schools, community college, and four-year college). When a given program cannot utilize a full-time instructor, sharing an instructor between two institutions is a practical solution.

2. Adjunct appointments of instructors from cooperating industries or other agencies and agreements for release time at specific periods. For example, winter term in agricultural communities is the main time for course attendance and is also slack time for agribusiness, thus providing employee release time (students and instructors).

3. Consortia approaches to grant development to improve programs and services that are mutually beneficial.

The concept of mutual benefits is the key to institutional collaboration. One cannot assume that every one is simply interested in the "good" of the community. Indeed, what is good for the community is always filtered through the legitimate self-interests of each organization within that community. The approach that makes everyone a winner makes the most sense. Introduction of new programs should not be at the expense of those currently existing. Instead, they should be complimentary; ideally, if interrelated by content or constituents, both programs should be enhanced. Constant communication and evaluation are needed to assure collaboration. Practitioners must advocate their programs and even their institutions, but not in a fashion that threatens the stability of other organizations in the community. If practitioners find themselves between their institutions' position and the legitimate interests of another organization, they may call for some form of informal mediation (if not in a position to undertake this personally). Task forces and advisory councils with broad representation can usually defuse any rivalries or misunderstandings if pulled into a problem early on and consulted at each point in the development of new programs.

Facilitating Communications: Learners, Staff, and Institution

Issues involving distance and isolation have been referred to often in this publication. In fact, sociologists of rural life often define a rural area as one that is by nature isolated parts served by some unifying structure. For an area to be rural, it must be isolated and also unified. Numerous communications problems can arise when outside institutions seek to serve dispersed rural populations.

1. Changes in planned events are difficult to communicate when people come from long distances. Simply posting a cancellation notice on a classroom door may be all right in a town where people travel less than a few miles to attend. However, if a person has driven more than 50 miles one way, left work early, and hired a baby-sitter, the cancellation or rescheduling of a program has larger consequences. It can especially dampen motivation for the newcomer to higher education. As a result, it is necessary to have more involved means of communication and to take more care in getting the prospective participants' work and home phone numbers, etc. Participants can also be provided with a toll-free telephone number to call in advance to determine if all arrangements are confirmed. Rural people often do this in the winter before driving; they call a road-report service. Why not provide a class-information service based on the same principle?

2. Credit and degree programs can face particular difficulty in adequately transmitting all needed information and explaining policies and procedures to the part-time rural adult learner. Regular campus forms and procedures usually need revision for off-campus delivery. Support services for registra-

tion, financial aid, and so on, are necessary when reaching out to the "uninitiated." As mentioned before, *oral* communication is what rural people rely on more than printed matter. A trained peer counselor who helps adults fill out forms can reduce their fears or anxieties much more effectively than even the most clearly stated and simple form letters, which go out to students in routine fashion to inform them of deadlines or deficiencies. These letters can be very disconcerting to part-time students distant from campus. Analysis of institutional form letters can produce enlightening results. Administrators may overlook the fact that a particular set of instructions includes the statement, "Stop by the campus bookstore to pick up your order form." The rancher 200 miles away may have difficulty complying with that instruction. On-campus students usually have on-campus advisers to whom they can turn, or other campus counselors, when they have a particular problem with the formal communications of the institution. Isolated adult learners may have no one to turn to when they receive a letter telling them they are "on probation" or "will be dropped unless . . . ." Young people often take such bureaucratic jargon in stride, but the older adult may be angered or otherwise discouraged by such communications. Having a known local person to check with is very important, as institutions cannot altogether eliminate their required forms and procedures.

3. Institutions and program coordinators have trouble keeping track of their adult learners, just as the learners have difficulty communicating with the institution. Some colleges today use computer terminals to maintain their communications. In one system each student is "logged-in" when she or he begins a particular educational event. The estimated time of completion, resources needed, and other pertinent information are also entered. As class assignments and other communications with the main campus or the learning center take place, they are all recorded or monitored or both. Progress checks are routinely made. If something is getting off schedule or if there is a problem it can be determined whether the problem is something in control of the student, the learning coordinator, or the institution. Steps can be made quickly to clarify and, it is hoped, get things back on track. If people have to alter their learning arrangements due to unforeseen circumstances, this, too, can be accommodated readily and future events planned without unnecessary backtracking or penalties to the student.

4. Newsletters to learners in rural areas are a useful device for providing information and also provide recognition for significant accomplishments of both learners and faculty alike. Newletters are one of the linking devices that provide the needed unity across the isolated rural communities. Feature stories in weekly newspapers are also important to maintain. These build good will and enhance the credibility of the programs.

5. In programs with multiple locations and staff, the care and feeding of

these off-campus personnel is of most importance. This is accomplished in different ways by different programs. Most programs provide at least quarterly in-service meetings for all who serve in the outreach program. Most also provide on-site consultation, where campus people visit the centers on a regular basis. Local coordinators will also develop their own local primary support group—usually three to five people with whom they have frequent contact as sounding boards and helpers. These functions of staff maintenance should not be assumed; rather, they must be openly discussed and planned for, to prevent burnout and to assure that such people are adequately trained and informed to carry out their assignments. Whenever possible, outreach personnel should have contact with other professionals from the main campus and be visibly recognized by that campus as part of the "family." This sense of affiliation is very important to outreach workers.

Use of Creative Strategies

The following are examples of creative outreach approaches that Mary Kinnick identified for the National Education Brokering Association (1981).

It is important for an agency to select the strategies it uses in light of its service capabilities (i.e., it is as debilitating to attract more clients than can be served effectively as it is to have few who use the services). Strategies should be targeted to the specific population(s) an agency is trying to reach (i.e., differentiate approaches to appeal/attract/motivate specific target populations). And, outreach strategies should be delivered in language and through media that will appeal to the target populations (i.e., avoid jargon and select delivery media that will be used by target populations). Remember, effective outreach strategies must not only make prospective clients aware of an agency's services but must also motivate them to take advantage of its services.

Listed below are examples of creative outreach approaches that have been used effectively by information and counseling service agencies.

Using media creatively to promote services

1. Use local newspapers, including neighborhood papers and "nickle ads," to publicize the agency's services. Human-interest feature stories on successful clients, particularly in local and neighborhood papers, will help clients clearly relate to the services (e.g., "I have the same background she did; maybe those people can help me get a job"). In rural areas, use the classified advertising section of the local paper to publicize the agency's services frequently, as well as using the feature-story approach.

2. Sell a local radio station on a weekly talk show, on which discussion deals with issues of importance to adults facing career and educational decisions. Discussions can focus on general trends and needs (e.g., problems adults face in making a career change); on current or impending events (e.g., results of recent career workshops for homemakers or an impending career workshop for the unemployed); on an interview with a client who has made a successful career change or re-enrolled in school; etc. Interviews with other service providers on a particular service they provide and how to access it is a possibility, too. (Make sure to know the times that the target populations are most likely to tune in to the radio station and get appropriate air time).

3. Persuade a local radio station to put on a weekly call-in show that gives career advice. The show can either be topically targeted (e.g., "this week we will answer questions on external degree opportunities") or generally oriented to refer callers to appropriate agencies for assistance or to offer general counsel or both.

4. Place a regular column in a local newspaper to offer readers career and educational advice. The column can focus on answering readers' questions (e.g., "Dear Abby" format) or take up a different issue of career and educational decision making.

5. Use spot advertisements for the agency's services on local radio stations. Generally, it is better to target spot ads to the particular populations wanted at the times they are most likely to be listening rather than to shotgun an entire listening audience.

6. Make a video tape or slide show that effectively illustrates the kinds of services provided and the kinds of people served. Make it available to various groups, such as schools, other agencies, service clubs, etc.

7. Sell a local commercial or cable television station on a human-interest show that portrays your services and those who may use them. All commercial stations have public service air time, and cable stations have public access requirements for air time and for the utilization of studio and equipment.

8. Run spot ads on local commercial or cable television to announce the services. Again, it is better to target the announcements to specific populations than it is to shotgun to listeners.

9. At the least, get periodic, if not frequent, media coverage of agency services in as substantive a form as you can sell to local programmers (e.g., guest spots on talk shows, public service announcements of major events).

10. In collaboration with other agencies and organizations, establish a toll-free inward WATS line and hire someone to advise callers on where to get assistance. Basic information can be provided directly, as well (e.g., "Where can I study dog grooming?" "When does the term start at Poco Poco State College?").

Effectively using mailers, brochures, and other matter to promote the agency's services

1. Have past clients design and write a mailer or brochure that aims at attracting others like themselves and, in their own words, explain how the agency's services helped them.

2. Send a mailer to former clients to keep them abreast of current activities. Word-of-mouth outreach initiated by former clients is still among the best strategies, and keeping former clients informed of activities will keep the agency fresh in their minds.

3. Put inserts and articles into company, union, and agency newsletters that feature someone from the given organization whom the agency has served.

4. Develop mailers targeted to specific audiences and distribute them through avenues sure to reach the particular target populations. Some examples of creative distribution strategies for mailers are:

- stuffed into grocery bags
- mailed with unemployment checks
- mailed with welfare checks
- mailed with electric, water, or telephone bills
- sent to those on mailing lists procured from special groups or organizations whose membership includes those the agency is trying to reach
- handed out by the county extension agents
- given out by Welcome Wagon staff or other community agents who make direct contact with individuals

When sending mailers accompanied by checks, make sure to state that it is not mandatory for recipients to report to the agency for service. Without such a disclaimer counseling may be overwhelmed by inquires initiated through compliance rather than actual interest in their services.

5. Send a brochure to key staff of other agencies and organizations who have contact with the group(s) to be served, encouraging them to refer clients to the agency.

6. Set-up display racks, put up posters, or leave copies of the agency's brochure or description sheets in places where people congregate. Have some kind of tear-off card that people can send in for more information and that allows them to express their interests in the services (people are more apt to reply if they get the chance to describe why they might want services related to their personal interests). Examples of places to set up racks and posters are banks, county fairs, other agencies and organizations, shopping centers and businesses, churches, bowling alleys, barber shops, beauty salons, and doctors' and dentists' offices.

7. Send a brochure or mailer aimed at homemakers via elementary

school students. They almost always make sure that material aimed at getting home gets there.

Building "natural neighbor" networks

1. Collaborate extensively with other agencies and organizations that are trying to serve the same populations the agency serves. Work with them jointly to sponsor and staff programs (e.g., workshops on career planning for homemakers; retraining opportunities for the unemployed).

2. Train as "referral agents" key members of the community who have contact with target populations. These might include bartenders, barbers, beauticians, and members of the clergy.

3. Establish working agreements with business and industry personnel offices to refer job applicants or laid-off employees to the agency for counseling assistance.

4. Disseminate small stickers with the agency's logo and phone number to agencies, community organizations, and others who work with the people to be reached. Ask that the sticker be affixed to their phones for easy reference and client referral.

5. Identify and establish personal communication with key individuals who are leaders or spokespersons in the communities. Among other things, these people can be involved in program planning or advisory committees and as actual outreach extensions for the organization.

6. Establish regular and permanent outreach sites where the target populations are likely to pass. For example, station a staff person at a table one afternoon a week at a union hall, day-care-center, an employment-service office, a shopping mall, a department or grocery store, or a post office. This strategy is most effective when people know that someone will be at the site at a prescribed time.

7. Have a local person or group sponsor a community open house or coffee at which members of the community are invited to talk with agency staff about service availability. Again, it is generally better to target a specific audience.

8. Get invited to make a presentation on agency services to local service clubs and organizations. Some of the possibilities are obvious, such as Rotary, Lions, and women's organizations. Others are less obvious, but nevertheless prospective, conduits for reaching those who less frequently take advantage of services, such as local "four-wheeler" or motorbike clubs, and CB groups. When possible, have a current or former client attend such presentations, too, to explain in her or his own words what services are offered.

9. Have the local library sponsor brown bag lunches at which the agency's services are discussed. Or have the library or other sites sponsor lunches with a special topic germane to one population or another (e.g.,

"Part-time Career Opportunities for Mothers"; "Working and Going to College—Some Alternatives"; "Basic Steps to Successfully Changing Jobs"). Participants generally seek more intensive assistance after these short, one-sided sessions.

Other useful strategies

1. Staff outreach efforts with people who are from the group(s) the agency is trying to reach. This might be done on a one-shot basis for a special program or event or on a long-term arrangement. In the latter case, outreach assistance might be received from target-group members on a volunteer basis, on a part-time employment basis, or through a cooperative work-experience or intern program if the person is enrolled in college.

2. Hold promotional events, such as conferences on career planning for Group X, career days, job fairs and college days. These kinds of one-time or annual events can be well publicized and held collaboratively with other agencies and schools, and promotional gimmicks can be used to help out busy people. Free records, tickets to sporting events, retail goods, or even a free college class might be solicited from local sponsors to promote the event and be given as door prizes.

3. Have clients put on improvisational street theater or musicales that both entertain onlookers and promote the services.

4. Collaborate with a local library, educational service district, or any other organization that has a mobile van. A staff person can ride along as an itinerant counselor or outreach worker.

5. Offer workshops at a variety of locations (schools, businesses, libraries, employment-service offices, etc.) to introduce people to the agency's services. Like brown-bag lunches described previously, this kind of session can either be general in nature or topical (e.g., "Planning Retirement Activities").

Characteristics of Effective Outreach Programs

The following is a summary of the major characteristics of a good outreach program as defined by rural students and facilitators attending a conference on rural programs, sponsored by "New Dimensions," the rural women's outreach project of the University of Idaho and Washington State University (Moscow, Idaho: April 19-20, 1983) that the author attended.

- has an effective means of reaching people and making them aware of opportunities
- assists individuals and groups with the sharing and development of their own skills

- utilizes *local* resources and groups and referral agents
- utilizes good information (free of jargon) that is honest and reliable with respect to program descriptions
- has flexibility—covers a wide range of individual needs and modes of participation
- offers programs that are enjoyable, stimulating, and even inspirational
- emphasizes programs that have short time frames (intensive)
- breaks down content of programs into small (bite-size) pieces
- offers programs that are practical, technically useful, and oriented to job skills
- provides coordination between different education providers and gives good information on differences in institutions and programs
- recognizes prior learning as legitimate, both in terms of academic credit and also as an aspect in all education and training (Prior consultation with any group for which an education event is planned is recommended to determine the prior background in the subject as well as current needs for information.)
- offers intergenerational learning opportunity
- offers programs for women only where and when appropriate to group needs
- gives awareness of the outside world through exposure to other cultures and ideas and to current regional, national, and world issues
- provides for coordination of room facilities, community-events calendars, etc., and avoids duplication and competition for scheduling time
- offers programs with nonstereotyped and bias-free approaches
- has a cost-effective delivery that incorporates all possible sources of funding, local and outside the community
- offers some programs strictly for personal improvement rather than for college credit or job training
- involves the total family unit in a significant number of educational programs
- makes certain that instructors know something about adult education
- utilizes technology effectively and efficiently and provides support or learning aids to television programs (including facilitating discussion-group formation, availability of tutors, etc.)
- utilizes approaches to programs that build participant self-esteem and personal confidence as a learner and rural citizen
- offers programs that lead to something—credentials or degrees—and are not unrelated fragments of programs or only partial degree requirements that necessitate going to campus for completion
- offers programs that contribute to the quality of life in the community, enriching the participants and bettering their understanding of their role in social change in rural towns

Issues for Postsecondary Institutions

Relating Institutional Mission to Rural Clientele

In the previous section the relationship of institutional mission to rural educational delivery was reviewed. Not all institutions have clearly defined their mission, although there are some general assumptions that apply to institution type. Community colleges in rural areas, for example, can generally be assumed to have service to adults as a major aim of their programs. In many sections of the country these colleges provide the only opportunity for higher education services within a 90- to 100-mile radius of their campuses. They perform services for the communities not available to the citizens of the geographic area through any other local public or private agency.

As John Eaton (1981) has written:

A community college represents an ideal catalyst for addressing many of the problems of rural life when solutions lie in the educational development of people. Consistent with the purposes of the community college are the initiation and implementation of programs and services that enhance educational, economic, cultural, recreational and civic development in rural areas.

During the past decade there has been increased development of community-based organizations that have specific missions in rural towns. Learning cooperatives using volunteers for noncredit programs, economic development agencies that provide training and assistance to individuals and small business ventures, and programs that target on specific populations such as displaced homemakers or developmentally disabled adults are examples of specific-purpose types of community-based groups. Their missions are clear, and, of course, their clientele groups are well defined.

Four-year colleges and universities exist in significant numbers across the country in rural communities. However, these institutions do not necessarily have a stated purpose in serving adult learning needs in the surrounding small towns. Large land grant universities will have a direct relationship to the Cooperative Extension Service for training programs of extension personnel and limited research activity, particularly in agricultural extension programs. Their staff will often travel around a state or region offering short-term workshops for adult skill development on a noncredit basis. This is a significant part of the total fabric of adult learning opportunity across the nation.

In the area of providing credit programs and extended degree opportunities for residents of small rural towns, four-year colleges and universities offering comprehensive programs are definitely in the minority. For the universities, research continues to dominate their institutional mission and on-campus teaching, which supports in large measure the institution's research staff and functions. There are neither incentives nor specific guidelines developed that would provide for significant institutional commitments of resources to remote locations.

Rural community colleges typically report a lack of interest from the state universities in providing courses or degree opportunities on an outreach basis. In some areas where campus enrollments have begun to decline, universities are cutting back the off-campus programs they had been offering, such as rural teacher training, and requiring people to attend on-campus in the summer. At the other extreme, in response to the same problem of on-campus attrition, some institutions have proliferated course offerings around the state with no cohesive planning, no local articulation effort, and often no credit toward degree programs (or the courses may all be electives, which still necessitates campus attendance for general education and the major field).

For four-year colleges and universities, off-campus instruction is often seen as "public service" rather than instruction (when relating this activity to institutional priority setting).

In the absence of specific institutional mission statements that relegate the provision of off-campus instruction to rural areas as an institutional priority, there is little room for optimism in the improvement of the haphazard delivery of continuing education programs. On the other hand, those institutions with four-year and graduate instruction that have made a clearly defined commitment to small communities and access to educational opportunity near where people live and work will be in a position to cooperate effectively with local colleges, school districts, employers, and other community-based organizations. It is hoped that they will also be in the favored position for obtaining state and federal funding assistance for projects to improve the quality of programs and to surmount barriers of rural delivery and access. It can be noted in the requests for proposals from the federal government, as well as from private foundations, that the issue of institutional mission clarification, with reference to proposed grant activities, is more and more common as a criterion for evaluation of a proposal's merit.

Once the mission is stated, particularly with reference to institutional commitment to rural people and their communities, then the other issue is that of appropriate roles and functions. The following are generally the types of roles the institution should fulfill.

1. direct provider of programs and services where no local agency has the resources or capability and where such programs are uniquely the domain or curricular allocation of the four-year college or university in that region

2. broker for rural communities to bring in needed programs or services that are not within the ability of that institution to provide directly but that can be obtained by it and transmitted to the point of identified need

3. collaborator in jointly offering programs and services in cooperation with other educational institutions, public agencies, or business and industry

Through the formation of local regional advisory committees, institutions outside the communities to be served can determine in an ongoing fashion which of the three primary roles they will need to serve in each particular situation. This vehicle for articulating a general institutional mission to the actual delivery of programs is indispensable for effective programming.

Establishing Delivery Systems

Once the issues surrounding institutional mission are addressed, the task of relating that mission to an appropriate system of educational delivery must be undertaken. Some delivery systems are logical extensions of the curricular mode. For example, correspondence study is obviously delivered through the mail. Televised courses are delivered over local cable television networks unless a particular rural area is not served by cable, in which case arrangements can sometimes be made to have video tapes of the programs mailed to central viewing centers. Of course, whether one is talking about correspondence study or public television instruction, there is the question of exactly how the rural adult was brought into contact with this resource in the first place and how the particular educational activity will be related to access to a degree or certification program. When discussing comprehensive delivery systems for rural areas, it is useful to think of literally all options available to the learner and to relate each option to the over-all display of opportunities, in order that participants can make informed judgments and practitioners can maximize resources and cost effectiveness.

There are a number of specific issues related to the establishment of rural educational delivery systems. The following is a discussion of four particularly important issues.

1. *Will the delivery system utilize local resources, or will it largely be externally developed and provided?* As previously mentioned, one might assume that programs offered on public television would not require local resources for their delivery. However, for the areas without public television access, a local agency equipped with video playback compatible with the college's own video formats will be needed to provide a viewing location for video tapes of the PBS broadcasts. The college itself will need some type of courier or mail service and duplication routine to accommodate the need. And, as is the case in virtually all effective programs for rural areas, local coordinators or program contact people are very important to inform people adequately of the courses, time and location of viewing, and arrangements they need to make with the college offering credit.

It is not within the scope of this book to provide a comprehensive review of all systems and details of their implementation. However, in addition to the example regarding the use of public television, a number of programs can be cited that are externally produced but cannot realistically reach a significant number of rural adults without a support delivery system based in the communities to be served. In the case of courses and workshops, there are obvious needs for spaces in which to meet. A college in Oklahoma describes a credit program offered in a taco restaurant's back room. A college in Oregon uses a local Chevrolet dealer to show video tapes of PBS courses on the dealer's showroom floor in the evenings. A rural sheriff's station had received some video equipment through a federal law enforcement grant but had no practical use for it. It found a college willing to video tape campus courses and send them by mail to the remote county location, where the deputies spent two evenings a week watching college classes.

Many educators believe that the most sophisticated technological system is the best. This may not always be the case. In Alaska a satellite demonstration project report concluded that it was only one way of providing telecommunications coverage. It was recommended that the village or regional people control the plans and curriculum for the educational programs that are taken by isolated rural students.

In Canada a very expensive television course for regional librarians was prepared and aired for 10 weeks throughout the country. Spot checks were made by telephone to determine number and retention of the audience. One location checked on had 12 people watching initially but no one watching at the fourth broadcast. A very fine and reputable professor just did not communicate well on television.

In the case of community-based adult education, the local delivery system is, of course, all important. Often, real innovation is called for in coming up with adequate resources in small towns. Small towns, by their nature, offer the local educational agency the opportunity to integrate all aspects of a community into a comprehensive system. This takes leadership skill because small towns have their own issues of turf and rivalry if not appropriately coordinated. Increasingly it has become important for community-based colleges and other educational organizations to expand their delivery system to include a brokering function of bringing in outside resources or tying in outside learning networks with their community or region. A school offering adult basic education finds its clientele hungry for postsecondary opportunities. The two-year degree person seeks a four-year degree opportunity, and once that is obtained, graduate training is desired. The result is an increasing need for institutional collaboration and effective information services provided to rural learners.

2. *Will the programs provided lend themselves to a unimodal or a multimodal delivery format?* The majority of university-produced instructional programs today that are offered to rural areas utilize a unimodal delivery format. That is, they rely exclusively on one instructional mode, such as radio, telephone instruction, live instructor in a local classroom, and so on. Very few institutions have developed multimodal delivery in which televised material is supplemented with, for example, telephone discussion and packaged independent study.

Most practitioners of adult and continuing education in rural areas have concluded that unimodal delivery systems are severely limited in their capacity to effectively reach, serve, and retain rural learners. For one thing, people in small towns enjoy the social interaction of a classroom. For another, they may have had little or no formal postsecondary learning, and they require more structure of their time than watching television at home or the pursuit of independent study provides. In some studies it has been reported that up to 90 percent of adults have left independent study courses without completing them.

The preferred multimodal delivery system will do two things. First, it will provide more than one option for a preferred learning style or orientation—audio, visual, visual-tactile, etc. For example, some people learn better by reading than they do by watching or by listening. Second, it will be interactive in some form—providing interaction between instructor and learner, learner and other learners. Some form of multiple options for interactions seems to be very important for the majority of rural learners' success.

3. *Will the programs foster interinstitutional collaboration?* Even though the growth of postsecondary educational programs for rural areas is not dramatic, what has been taking place has inevitably run into the issue of "intersegmental impact." That is, local people may desire that a four-year college offer its programs in the area of a community college. But the local college may not be comfortable with what it perceives as competition for enrollments. Graduate studies will be more accepted than undergraduate programs, some of which may be borderline as to whether they are upper-division or lower-division offerings. Also, there are limited instructional resources in the local area, and an outside college that bases its program on local resources (as contrasted to imported faculty) does present a possible threat to resource availability. A good example is practicum sites for colleges: with only one hospital or only one forest-service office, there are obvious limitations on the number of practicum students that can be accommodated. Competition for these desirable slots can cause problems if not carefully coordinated.

As previously mentioned, where there is more than one postsecondary institution offering programs, interagency agreements are required to avoid misunderstandings and problems of perceived competition. More important, resources and creative approaches to joint programming need to be shared. Most interagency agreements will spell out the role and mission of each party to the agreement, the services each will provide as primary provider and options for secondary provision, the name and location of a liaison administrator responsible for articulation of his or her organization's part of the agreement with the other liaison people from participating agencies, and a clearly understood process for addressing possible problems in implementing the agreement (this typically implies senior administrators as the next line of response if a liaison staff person cannot bring an issue to resolution; without this the staff person can get hopelessly caught up in the other organization's bureaucracy).

To reduce or eliminate duplication of services most programs will have quarterly or annual planning sessions in which proposed schedules are shared and resources are coordinated. They will also announce the co-sponsorship of programs that are coordinated in order to assure the public of nonduplication of efforts.

Unfortunately, the majority of rural educators feel that universities from outside their local areas are not at all sensitive to concerns about program coordination. There appears to be great need to improve collaboration and communications with the various providers of programs across state and regional lines.

4. *What are the institutional capacity and the cost efficiency of the program?* Institutional mission and the type of educational delivery system to be used will establish definite parameters for what kind of particular educational programs can be offered. The range and scope of programs is further defined by interinstitutional agreements and by the guidance of local advisory committees. No doubt the largest single determinant of programming is the institution's own capacity to develop, promote, deliver, and finance any particular program.

Many rural practitioners and small-college administrators complain that they do not have adequate models on which to base their program development efforts. Professional association meetings and conferences are typically dominated by large institutions, very often urban based, that display working models not directly applicable to a rural setting nor to small-scale enterprises.

What may be required is something akin to the so-called homegrown or garden-variety approach to program development. In this mode one does not think exclusively of large-scale development nor of sophisticated technology and high-cost resources. Instead, there is the tendency to get the job done in the most expedient manner with the least cost of time and resources. For example, it has been found that certain lecture-oriented classes that have been video-taped for distance learners can be followed equally well by many people in an audio cassette format. The audio cassette is much more portable and can be listened to "while I do my ironing" or "in the truck on the way to work." In another example, it was found that reading and conference arrangement on a campus, in which a student studies a text and course outline independently and has two of three conferences with the professor, can be offered externally, with the conference taking place over the telephone instead of in the office.

There are many examples of creative use of teaching and learning resources in the homegrown mode. Additional examples include a brief radio discussion series in a talk-show format followed by reading assignments printed in the local newspaper; small study support groups that take lessons out of programs such as the Great Decisions program and work with a college professor as a distance mentor; use of high school teachers as mentors for materials produced by college professors, the mentors having been brought to the campus in the summer for a thorough orientation to the course materials before being approved as adjunct faculty; and adults contracting for their own designed learning experiences with local experts and distant college mentors (similar to cooperative education contracts in business and industry).

The key to rural program development is *flexibility*. Faculty and administrators of postsecondary institutions will find they have many more options than they originally envisioned for program development if they will be flexible and creative in their approach. This is especially true if their organization has made effective arrangements with local resource networks and if the adult clientele has been effectively mobilized to assist in the determination of appropriate learning packages and experiences.

While it would appear that this approach will have the most promise for the majority of locally developed options, this is not to say that the large scale regional or national opportunities—such as public radio, television, and correspondence study—are to be ruled out. Quite the contrary. What is needed is a way to incorporate the best of all options into the most workable program development effort.

Institutional Policies and Administration

Whether considering problems of local, small, community-based colleges or programs extended from institutions outside the local area, there are major policy issues to face when attempting to reach isolated adults with educational programs. First and foremost is the question of the commitment of resources. Of course, institutional mission is totally involved in the issue of resource commitment. For the local community college in a rural area, the mission is usually more clear than for the university sending out faculty through an outreach program. However, in both cases there has been some prior determination of whether or not the off-campus adult student will be served with the same level of resource commitment or whether or not such clientele must be self-supporting. Boyd (1983) puts the issue in an interesting context when he writes:

> Is the expenditure necessary to equip and operate a university basketball team merited (for only five players)? Is supplying a professor on campus for a class of seven graduate students merited? I assume, based on practice, that the answer to each is "yes." I am led to believe, therefore, that true merit has less to do with quantitative results and more to do with qualitative potential. . . . The quesiton is one of commitment to (rural) education, not merit nor number of students.

When programs offered by colleges and universities for rural delivery are primarily numbers driven, where program developers are on a pay-your-own-way basis or even expected to generate surplus income for the university, then efforts will clearly be limited to the kinds of activities that have high ability to pay—mostly the areas of business, industry, or professional workshops. It is not likely that degree programs or vocational or professional training programs that are tied to the developing needs of small rural communities will be largely addressed with an income-generating approach. Also, it is not likely that sustained commitment to follow through with the needs of people in longer-range career goals will be evidenced, as the income-generating efforts tend to be one-shot programs that have no long-range commitment attached.

Another issue that is directly related to mission is the question of how institutional personnel and resources are managed in the delivery of off-campus instruction. How are faculty compensated and professionally recognized for their involvement with rural communities? How are department resources integrated with on-campus and off-campus activities? How are student support services, such as financial aid, career and academic advisement, etc., extended to the part-time off-campus student (if at all)? (Many older students, especially single parents, have a great need for financial aid when returning to college. Their participation in the college financial program significantly reduces the availability of funds for 18- to 22-year-old students that the college is likely to be actively recruiting.) Is there equity or inequity in quality, access, and service?

Perhaps the single most important administrative issue is whether programs serving off-campus rural learners will be integrated into the total institutional fabric or whether the programs will be free standing or institutions unto themselves. There are few institutions among four-year colleges and universities that have adopted an integrated model, whereas this tends to be the rule rather than the exception for community colleges. Alternatives to institutional integration include establishing special branches or units within institutions that have rural service as their major focus and requisite flexibility designed into their institutional procedures; free-standing institutions that yet draw on system resources, such as Empire State College in New York; or as-yet-untried measures such as providing leverage, through special funding, to a rural oversight board within the institutions, which would then assure that rural clients were served through the university system resources.

Regardless of the pattern of organization adopted, most rural colleges having success in developing their mission to serve place-bound adults are doing so with some degree of external funding assistance. Higbee and Stoddard (1981) discuss development efforts in an article for the *Journal of the American Association of Community and Junior Colleges*. They conclude that there are three important ingredients in obtaining support funding.

- *Needs* must be real and identifiable.
- *Vision* must be evidenced to see how the additional resources will positively affect students and the institution alike.
- *Courage* or reasonable risk-taking must be evidenced by the chief administrator(s) to provide adequate personnel and operational dollars from already-limited funds.

Finally, small rural colleges do have unique organizational problems that must be addressed. As Charles Atwell (1981) has observed:

> First of all, many of the basic principles of organization upon which our bureaucracies are built either do not apply at all to the small rural setting or are so different in application that they become unrecognizable.

In a small college the number of functional areas to be administered far exceeds the number of administrators available. What is needed may be a generalist approach to management coupled with more reliance on paraprofessional assistance (where larger institutions would rely on professional staffing). By taking these two approaches to staffing and by arranging for the kind of interinstitutional and interagency agreements referred to previously, small colleges have some attainable economies of administration that can still be effective. If small colleges do their homework in curtailing their own operating costs and provide effective programs for rural citizens, they are very likely to find the people in small towns more than willing to find ways to undergird the colleges' efforts with various forms of local support.

Issues for National and State Policy

Speaking primarily about elementary and secondary school programs and policy issues, Everitt Edington (1980) wrote:

> The education reforms of this century have generally overlooked the special problems of the rural portion of the society. . . . Policies regarding education have been primarily developed for all schools and all children, ignoring the fact that there may be vastly different needs associated with educating people in the rural areas of the country.

In the late 1970s and early 1980s, the United States has witnessed an upsurge of interest in its rural areas and economic development; however, the role of education finds little mention. Rural America suffers from neglect, disorganization, and lack of federal rural development policy. Because rural schools and colleges are so central to their communities' total character and identity, community development cannot be accomplished apart from education. Also, to improve education in rural areas one cannot undertake such improvement by working exclusively on the school. Rural communities, rural society, the supporting agencies for education, and, in fact, total society must be taken into account.

We have seen that, in the past, the United States has taken a definite interest in and has made concerted federal policy decisions regarding rural interests. At the time of the Morrill Act, which as early as 1863 developed the land grant university system in the nation, there was federal attention to rural areas. But at that time, 75 percent of the population lived in rural communities, the majority on farms. The Cooperative Extension Services was born out of the Smith-Lever Act of 1914, and in 1917, the Smith-Hughes Act provided for federally financed vocational education. The latter act recognized that agriculture was an extremely important industry in the nation and developed programs for financing vocational agriculture in rural schools. These three major federal initiatives and the majority of other national policies have been fairly narrow in definition by looking at the farming and agriculture sector, which today represents less than 15 percent of the nonurban population. In addition, these policies did not coordinate with other rural policies, thus separating the important function of education from the other social and economic programs in the rural communities.

Within the past decade, there have been a number of policy statements issued by federal- and state-supported task forces and commissions on issues in rural education. These bodies have generally concentrated on elementary and secondary education. Postsecondary education is sometimes mentioned but has not, as yet, been a focus. The administrations of Kennedy, Johnson, and Carter commissioned studies and reports on rural education; however, there is little evidence that any of the policies recommended in these studies has been nationally implemented.

The Rural Development Act of 1972 attempted to coordinate policy but, in actual practice, failed to do so. Funds from this act went to the land grant universities in each state. The presidents of the universities had the responsibility for disbursement of funds. In the majority of cases, the funds were passed on to the dean of the college of agriculture and the extension and research programs, which are, for the most part, in the colleges of agriculture. Because of the biases inherent in a discipline, development in rural America has tended to be limited to that of agricultural or economic development.

Special rural populations have also been the focus of policy statements issued by federal and state agencies. In 1977 the U.S. Office of Education developed recommendations on rural, migrant Native American and bilingual, bicultural education. The National Task Force on Instructional Strategy in Schools with High Concentration of Low-Income Pupils recognized that the cultural traditions of rural society can create difficulties in developing policy for rural students. Again, as with other policy statements, little has been done to provide funding and program development support to implement strategies based on the policies.

There is need for policies at the federal and state level that differentiate between urban and rural areas in education. There is need to develop a policy for the 1980s that recognizes that community development and rural education are viewed in their totality and interrelationship. There is need for a specific focus on rural postsecondary education at the community, regional, state, and federal level; and that focus must also be drawn out of the total context of economic development and learning opportunities for all ages.

Issues at the National Level

Although there have been numerous policy statements prepared, there is need for a comprehensive policy that overcomes the many shortcomings of the recent past and also becomes enacted in legislation and executive order. In the area of policy formation, rural distinctions are particularly evident in the issues relating to *equity* and *appropriateness*. Rosenfeld (1981) has written the following:

> Equity, to the extent that it is a constitutional issue, is a direct object of federal policy. Federal and state policy makers are faced with creating the funding mechanisms and regulations to ensure equitable support for rural districts and services for individuals with special needs. Appropriateness, however, is a function of local conditions and community preferences. Therefore, forms of services and kinds of programs are influenced by, not controlled by, current federal policies.

In attempts to provide equity, too much emphasis has been placed at the federal level on the "numbers game." Rural educators charge that federal criteria for allocations of educational dollars are negatively biased to the detriment of nonurban communities. The measurement criteria for educational programs using federal monies include relative wealth of an area, concentration of poverty, economic conditions, and willingness to introduce new programs in line with national priorities. Practitioners say that rural property values, for instance, tend to be inflated with respect to income and that rural unemployment statistics have been shown to be mistakenly low. Rural and isolated areas with small numbers of people who are sometimes widely dispersed present educators with delivery costs far exceeding the costs in areas where populations are concentrated and accessible. For program delivery, equivalent dollars based on per-pupil formulas do not generate equivalent resources, especially when one considers the high cost of transporting either instructional resources of students to and from the colleges as well as lower student–instructor ratios.

In the allocation of federal monies to the states, the federal government should establish guidelines other than population-based criteria for meeting rural needs. Set-asides, entitlements, and catch-up funding formulas have been recommended as a way to provide more equity, particularly when putting block grant programs into effect. Federal assistance has been disproportionately allocated between rural and urban populations for educational programs, but this is not solely a function of inadequate formulas. Size of scale and availability of local resources for matching and developing funding applications are very real barriers. Studies have shown that many eligible participants among schools and colleges do not pursue available federal programs because they do not have the staff to develop competitive proposals; lack matching funds often required; or cannot, due to size of scale, produce results with relatively small amounts of assistance. Many colleges also consider the burden of compliance with federal and state regulation too heavy when compared to the potential income.

The financing of rural education cannot be borne exclusively by rural citizens. State and federal agencies need to provide assistance while allowing rural people maximum latitude in determining their own needs and priorities. Present and pending policies should be examined to eliminate not only funding inequity but also discrimination against, or neglect of, rural populations through *antirural bias*. Several sociologists have commented on this major problem associated with developing a rural policy. They say problems of day-to-day life in rural society are emotionally invisible in contrast to the highly dramatic problems of the city. And when rural people do surface in a national consciousness, it is too often in a stereotypical form.

As Cosby (1980) points out, the labels "hicks," "red-necks," "plowboys," "hillbillies," "crackers," and "clodhoppers" and others equally degrading are often used to describe rural people, but no such comparable list exists for urban dwellers.

> When "hicks" are not driving tractors or picking hayseeds out of their hair, they are voting for conservative candidates, chewing tobacco, quilting, square dancing, swatting flies or coon hunting. Similar "humorous" images represent activities of most rural institutions, including schools, law enforcement, religion, health care and government. The evaluative characteristics of rural images can be easily distilled into a dichotomy between "urban equals superior" and "rural equals inferior."

Television, of course, has been capitalizing on the humorous emphasis, and most urban dwellers (including the majority of federal policy makers) are exposed to rural America through "Hee Haw," "The Dukes of Hazzard," and "Petticoat Junction." This view is like the Amos and Andy depiction of the plight of black Americans—but the national consciousness has not made a similar transition of perspective. The result is that even though more than 60 million people live in rural communities, their real needs and problems are rarely taken seriously by government or by the intellectual and scientific communities of the nation.

The other problem with the context of federal policy making, even among those who are most sympathetic and sensitive to rural concerns, is one of local generalizing—the tendency to assume that *rural* means the same thing across America or a certain sameness depending on one's own orientation. For example, the New Englander has her or his own view of rural America, as does the Midwesterner, the Southerner, and the Westerner. But there are tremendous differences across the nation's regions; there is, perhaps, more pluralism in the countryside than within the cities.

It must be recognized in federal policy that there are vast cultural differences in rural America and that there are a number of minirural cultures spread throughout the land. The rural black culture is extremely different in the South from what it is in the the Midwestern farm population. The Hispanic culture in the West is very different from that of the Indians of Alaska or the Western-ranch Anglo population. The pockets of Appalachian poverty are different from rural pockets of affluence, such as ski resort communities in the West.

Assumptions among policy makers about homogenization are very prevalent, despite the vast social and economic differentiation of rural areas. Also, many decision makers still believe that urbanism is the wave of the future and that ruralism is declining, even though, as has been pointed out, this is no longer true. And, as has also been stated, the focus on agriculture of national policy persists as many people in Washington, D.C., still connect the concept of *rural* with *farm*. The U.S. Department of Agriculture still remains, in the early 1980s, the chief vehicle for addressing rural development programs and has been the official cosponsor, with the Department of Education, of most rural educational initiatives in the policy area.

A better mechanism is needed for policy input at the federal level from rural educators. Since the primary responsibility for education, including higher education, rests with the states, federal agencies should strongly encourage states to strengthen their programs for isolated and rural students. Interventions that encourage and develop better programs for youth and adults in rural communities should benefit from federal incentives in funding allocations.

Federal efforts should be expanded to develop and utilize communications technology for rural education delivery, including incentives to business and industry as well as direct government assistance in the acquisition of equipment and training resources.

Finally, little is known about rural education at this time. The federal government should provide for the systematic collection, compilation, and analysis of the status of participation in rural adult education. The large rural constituency has little or no voice in federal policy. There is a need to develop a means of involving rural people more directly in policy making at all levels of government.

Issues for State Policies

There are over a thousand small, rural two- and four-year colleges in the United States and hundreds more that serve, in part, a rural constituency. These institutions, together with thousands of community-based organizations and agencies for education, are in need of improved policies at the state level that will recognize their unique concerns.

A national survey was undertaken in 1980 by the Small Rural College Commission of the American Association of Community and Junior Colleges (AACJC). Of the respondents from the 50 states, 28 replied that small size of institution was compensated for or given consideration in their state funding formula or appropriation. However, only 5 states apparently recognize rural environment *per se* in their funding formulas. These are Maryland, Michigan, Nevada, New Hampshire, and Wyoming. The AACJC report (Williams, 1981) states:

> In 22 other states, officials, for varied reasons, have blatantly chosen not to confront the fiscal economies of scale issue, or have naively neglected to consider the financial realities facing the rural two-year institutions. Nonetheless, the concerns and problems do exist, and will perpetuate and become compounded unless significant constructive long-range fiscal solutions are enacted in all states. Without such vision, as inflation rates increase costs exponentially, and enrollment-driven flat funding formulas are utilized, the small/rural two-year institutions will no longer be able to fulfill the mission of serving the local postsecondary education needs.

In most states, one of the keys to a more equitable approach to supporting rural schools and colleges is regionalization within the state. Most states are highly centralized in their administrative and policy-making activities, and they impose statewide guidelines that do not usually differentiate rural and urban needs. Allowance must be made for regionalization or for planning that is derived from local initiative and not statewide overviews.

Many of the concerns expressed about views of federal officials toward rural areas pertain to state-level officials. Policy makers and agency officials need to be sensitized to local rural concerns. Rural educators should provide information through forums, media campaigns, testimony before legislatures, and other means. Rural consumers themselves need to be activated to lobby on their own behalf. Rural concerns as they apply to adult education needs should be clearly articulated in state plans, and resources should not be allocated solely by population formulas.

In states where high schools, community colleges, state colleges or universities, and other publicly funded educational agencies all manifest a presence in a given rural region, the state should play a more active role in managing cooperation. States need to develop policies that reward programs that cooperate in cost-saving efficiencies and collaborative educational efforts. State commissions need to play a more aggressive role in this regard in most states. State policies and programs that promote turf maintenance between schools and colleges should be confronted and revised or eliminated.

The states should also prioritize the development of communications from state capital to rural constituents. There is a rural political lag—leaders and educators have not been able to mobilize rural people to have an impact on state governments. When states have revenue shortfalls, regional offices are the first to be closed, while centralized functions are maintained near current levels. Small rural colleges, unable to maintain enrollment levels at the same ratio of instructors to students, fixed costs to tuition, etc., are prime targets for reduction or closure. The affected small communities have less dramatic impact on state-level politics, and citizens of the rest of the state can be reassured that "if those people really wanted all the benefits of adult education, they wouldn't live out there in isolation."

As has been stated earlier, this is, of course, a giant myth. Rural people do want access to postsecondary education and, as Marjorie Walker says, a say in what is provided.

> Having a say is a political as well as an educational issue. It bespeaks the right to participate in the planning, to contribute to the definition of programs and processes, to take part in the evaluation of the outcomes. Rural residents want to be assured that the educational services offered in their communities respond . . . to their priorities and needs (Mayrling, 1981, p. 4).

Another issue for the states is in the area of reciprocity for state funding of out-of-state students. Because many rural small towns exist in border relationships to other states and thereby form natural regional communities of an interstate nature, it is particularly important to provide access based on natural geographical configurations rather than on artificial state lines. The rationale for a policy of reciprocity should be consumer based and not largely institution based.

In addition to these major issues, individual states confront multiple problems in responding adequately to the needs of their educational programs for rural areas. Coordination is needed not only within the larger educational community but also with the private sector, business and industry, and all agencies concerned with social and economic development. Without specific policies for rural concerns, states will continue to be dominated by policies that have an urban and suburban bias. It is extremely important that states recognize the unique problems of rural areas, which are due primarily to geographic isolation and small numbers of students enrolling in desired programs and services. Since the primary responsibility for educational policy rests with the state, in cooperation with the local communities, the state is where the thrust of new efforts of advocacy must begin.

A Rural Postsecondary Action Agenda

In June 1981 the Fund for the Improvement of Postsecondary Education supported a 3-day working session at which 28 rural educators from around the nation gathered to examine rural adult education. This group, meeting in Kansas City, Missouri, developed a rural postsecondary action agenda, which reads as follows.

1. Establish a permanent professional alliance that will serve as a clearinghouse for adult rural education.
2. Advocate an institute for small, rural, educational institutions.
3. Undertake a comprehensive national study of rural adults and their educational needs.
4. Design strategies to focus national media on rural educational needs.
5. Undertake consciousness raising about rural concerns in local regions.
6. Develop a means of making useful connections with educational telecommunications projects around the country.
7. Establish a steering group to plan for professional development activities among rural postsecondary educators.
8. Stimulate rural postsecondary education publications through professional organizations.
9. Develop rural-concerns advocacy in professional associations.
10. Develop contact sources for funding rural programming.
11. Develop ways to disseminate ongoing progress.

If the level of commitment and determination of the 28 people gathered in Kansas City is any indication of the quality of professional involvement among rural educators generally (and we believe it is indicative), then these action items on their agenda will be pursued in the near future across the nation. There is no question about whether or not policies are needed at the state and federal levels to address the concerns of rural people. There is no question about whether or not innovative practices are in evidence that are successfully overcoming barriers to educational opportunity; these practices need wide dissemination and adoption (with local modification). There is no question that a new rural consciousness is dawning in this country that is highly influenced and shaped by educational endeavors. The greatest challenge facing rural educators today is the development of a strong rural constituency—rural advocates—to bring greater influence to bear in their legitimate self-interest. The time to address the challenges of rural postsecondary education is now.

References

Aker, G. F., et al. *Evaluation of an Adult Basic Education Program in a Southern Rural Community.* Tallahassee: Florida State University, 1968.

Atwell, C. A. "Doing More with Less." *Journal of the American Association of Community and Junior Colleges,* October 1981, p. 30.

Best, David. *Human Services in the Rural Environment,* vol. 3, no. 10. Madison, Wisconsin: University of Wisconsin, October 1978.

Beale, Calvin. *The Revival of Population Growth in Nonmetropolitan America.* Economic Research Service, ERS-605 Washington, D.C.: U.S. Department of Agriculture, June 1975.

Bishop, C. E., et al. *The People Left Behind.* Washington, D.C.: National Advisory Committee on Rural Poverty, 1976.

Boyd, Robert H. "Where Two or Three Are Gathered," *Continuum,* NUCEA Journal, Washington, D.C., 1983 (in press).

Bruce, R. L. *Adult Education for Rural Americans.* Columbus: Ohio State University; ERIC, 1979.

Bruce, R. L. *Designing Involvement.* Ithaca, New York: Cornell University, 1979.

Bureau of the Census, U.S. Department of Commerce, *Statistical Abstract of the United States: 1980.*

Carpenter, Edwin A. "The Potential for Population Dispersal: A Closer Look at Residential Location Preferences." *Rural Sociology* 42 (1977): p. 352.

Carter Administration. *Small Community and Rural Development Policy.* December 20, 1979, p. 1.

Clarenbuch, Kathryn. *Educational Needs of Rural Women and Girls,* Washington, D.C.: National Advisory Council of Women's Education Program, 1977.

Cosby, A. G. "The Urban Context of Rural Policy," *The Interstate Compact for Education,* Fall 1980, vol. XIV, no. 3, p. 39.

Dejong, G. F. "Selected Characteristics of Metropolitan to Non-metropolitan Area Migrants: A Study of Population Redistribution," *Rural Sociology* 41 (1976): p. 526.

Eaton, John M. "Small Rural Colleges: A Vital Component of the Delivery System," *Community and Junior College Journal,* October 1981, p. 15.

Edington, E. "Rural Education: Key Policy Issues," *The Interstate Compact for Education,* Fall 1980, vol. XIV, no. 3, p. C-1.

Fratoe, F. A. *Rural Education and Rural Labor Force in the Seventies.* Rural Development Research Report No. 5, U.S. Department of Agriculture, October 1978.

Glenn, N. D. and Hill, L., Jr. "Rural–Urban Differences in Attitude and Behavior in the United States," *The Annals* 429 (1977): pp. 36–50.

Goudy, Willis. "Evaluation of Local Attributes and Community Satisfaction in Small Towns," *Rural Sociology* 42 (1977): pp. 371–382.

Halfvarson, L. R., and O'Connor, J. A. *A Survey of Adult and Continuing Music Education in Illinois.* Urbana: University of Illinois, 1970.

Higbee, J. M., and Stoddard, R. K. "Paving the Way to Prosperity," *Journal of the American Association of Community and Junior Colleges,* October 1981, p. 23.

Knowles, Malcolm. *The Modern Practice of Adult Education.* Chicago: Follett Company, 1980, p. 20.

Lewis, Ray. *Guide to Educational Delivery Systems Using Telecommunications.* Washington, D.C.: AAHE, 1983 (in press).

Margolis, Richard. *Proceedings: The National Invitational Meeting on Rural Postsecondary Education.* Manhattan: Kansas State University, 1981.

Martorana, S. and Broomwell, J. "Survey Report: Legislation for Special Groups," *Journal of the American Association of Community and Junior Colleges,* 52:4, 42–44.

Meeting Learners' Needs through Telecommunications: A Directory and Guide to Programs. Washington, D.C.: AAHE, 1983.

Minnesota Research Coordinating Unit for Vocational Education. *A Study of the Needs for Occupational Recertification in Minnesota.* St. Paul, Minnesota: November 1982.

Mogey, John. "Recent Changes in the Rural Communities of the United States," *Sociologia Ruralis* 16 (1976): 139–160.

National Advisory Committee on Rural Poverty. Report to the Carter Administration, December 1976.

National Center for Education Statistics. *Participation in Adult Education,* 1981 edition. Washington, D.C., 1982.

Rogers, D. L., and Whiting, L. R., eds. *Aspects of Planning for Public Services in Rural Areas.* Ames: Iowa State University Press, 1976.

Rosenfeld, Stuart. *A Portrait of Rural America: Conditions Affecting Vocational Education Policy.* Vocational Education Study Publication No. 6, U.S. Department of Education, April 1981.

Shea, K. P. "American Agriculture: Who Stole the Revolution?" *Environment* 19 (1976): pp. 28–38.

Sher, J., ed. *Education in Rural America: A Reassessment of Conventional Wisdom.* Boulder, Colorado: Westview Press, 1977.

Smith, R. M., et al. *Handbook of Adult Education.* New York: MacMillan Co., 1970.

Summers, G. F. "Industrial Development of Rural America: A Quarter Century of Experience." *Journal of Community Development Society* 8 (1977): pp. 6–18.

Swanson, Louis E. et al. "Factors Influencing Willingness to Move: An Examination of Nonmetropolitan Residents." *Rural Sociology* 44: 719–35, Winter 1979.

Taylor, L., and Jones, A. R. *Rural Life and Urbanized Society.* New York: Oxford University Press, 1964.

TenHoeve, T., Jr. "To Serve Even the Last Man in Line." *Journal of the American Association of Community and Junior Colleges,* October 1981, pp. 17–19.

U.S. Department of Agriculture. *Rural America: Poverty and Progress—Rural Development Policy Issues,* Washington, D.C., December 1977.

U.S. Department of Education. *Adult Education Programs That Work in Rural Areas.* Washington, D.C.: Office of Adult and Vocational Education, 1980.

U.S. Department of Education. *Report of the National Task Forces on Instructional Strategy in Schools with High Concentration of Low Income Pupils.* Washington, D.C., 1977.

Walker, M. "Issues in Rural Education," a paper presented to the National Invitational Meeting on Rural Postsecondary Education, Fund for the Improvement of Postsecondary Education. Kansas City, Missouri, 1981, p. 3.

Williams, A. "Survey of Findings of the Study Comparing College Funding." *Journal of the American Association of Community and Junior Colleges* (October 1981), p. 45.

Practitioners' Library

Adult Education Newsletter. Montclair State College, Montclair, New Jersey.

Bulletin! National Center for Educational Brokering, 1211 Connecticut Ave., N.W., Suite 400, Washington, D.C. 20036.

Community-Based Programs That Work. Valencia Community College, P.O. Box 3028, Orlando, Florida 32802.

Course Trends in Adult Education. Lifelong Learning Resources, University of Kansas, 1221 Thurston, Manhattan, Kansas 66502.

Directory of Adult-Serving Programs. U.S. Department of Education, Office of Adult Learning and Community Education, Washington, D.C., 1981.

Directory of Educational and Career Information Services for Adults. National Center for Educational Brokering, 1211 Connecticut Avenue, N.W., Suite 400, Washington D.C. 20036.

Directory of Rural Organizations. National Rural Center, 1828 L Street, N.W., Washington, D.C. 20036.

Eastern Oregon Network. Eastern Oregon State College, La Grande, Oregon 97850.

External Degree Programs in the West. Western Interstate Commission on Higher Education, Boulder, Colorado, 1976.

Guide to Educational Delivery Systems Using Telecommunications. AAHE, Washington, D.C. (1983, in press).

Guide to Undergraduate External Degree Programs in the U.S., 1980. American Council on Education, 1 Dupont Circle, Washington D.C. 20036.

Ideas and Resources for Your Community. Small Towns Institute, Box 517, Ellensburg, Washington 98926.

Innovation Abstracts. National Institute for Staff and Organization Development, University of Texas at Austin.

The Learning Connection. Lifelong Learning Resources, University of Kansas, 1221 Thurston, Manhattan, Kansas 66502.

Lifelong Learning for Adult Years: Journal of Adult Education Association of U.S., Washington D.C.

New Directions for Continuing Education: Reaching Hard to Reach Adults, No. 8, Gordon G. Darkenwald and Gordon A. Larson, eds. Jossey-Bass, San Francisco, California, 1980.

Resources for Change: A Guide to Projects. Fund for the Improvement of Postsecondary Education, U.S. Department of Education, Washington, D.C.

Resources for Continuing Education Managers, Deans, and Directors. Bureau of Business and Technology, Inc., New York, New York.

Rural Development Programs: A Citizen's Action Guide. Center for Community Change, 1000 Wisconsin Avenue, N.W., Washington, D.C. 20007.

Rural Education News. Rural/Regional Education Association, 1201 6th Street, N.W., Washington, D.C. 20036.

Rural Educational Review. Eastern Oregon State College, La Grande, Oregon 97850.

Rural Education Programs That Work. U.S. Department of Education, Office of Vocational and Adult Education, Washington, D.C., 1980.

Rural Health Newsletter. National Rural Center, 1828 L Street, N.W., Washington, D.C. 20036.

The Rural and Small Town Community Education Manual. University for Man, 1221 Thurston, Manhattan, Kansas 66502.

Southern Appalachian Road Report. West Virginia Institute of Technology, Montgomery, West Virginia 25136.

Technological Horizons in Education Journal. Information Synergy, Inc., Acton, Massachusetts.

Telescan. The Digest of the Center for Learning and Telecommunication. American Association for Higher Education, 1 Dupont Circle, Washington, D.C.

Books of Interest from the College Board

Adult Access to Education and New Careers: A Handbook for Action. Carol B. Aslanian, project director, and Harvey B. Schmelter, editor. Shows postsecondary institutions how to design, operate, and evaluate an adult career counseling center. (001257) 1980, 141 pages, $9.75.

Adult Learning, Higher Education, and the Economics of Unused Capacity. Howard Bowen. Explores some major policy options for higher education during the next two decades and observes that accommodating increasing numbers of adults will become a very attractive choice. (237414) 1980, 33 pages, $4.

Americans in Transition: Life Changes as Reasons for Adult Learning. Carol B. Aslanian and Henry M. Brickell. Reports the results of a national study of 2,000 Americans 25 years old or older that was conducted in order to explain the causes and timing of adult learning. Useful to educational providers, planners, and counselors. (001273) 1980, 172 pages, $6.50.

Learning Times, Second Issue, Fall 1982. A lively, informative newspaper designed to start adults thinking about the diverse educational opportunities and resources available to them. (248101) 1982, 12 pages, $12 per package of 50 copies. No other discounts apply.

Senior Learning Times, Fall 1981. An informative publication geared to older adults who are interested in learning about various educational opportunities and resources. (248102) 1981, 12 pages, $15 per package of 50 copies. No other discounts apply.

Paying for Your Education: A Guide for Adult Learners. Contains complete, up-to-date national information designed to help adult learners obtain the financial aid for which they may be eligible. (001524) 1983, 140 pages, $7.95.

Independent Scholarship: Promise, Problems, and Prospects. Ronald Gross and Beatrice Gross. The findings and recommendations of a major, two-year project intended to identify and help meet the needs of America's independent scholars. (001648) 1983, 68 pages, $7.95.

Improving Financial Aid Services for Adults: A Program Guide. Ronald H. Miller, editor. Discusses the state of the art in financial aid services for adult learners and contains a selected, annotated bibliography for financial aid personnel working with adults. (238803) 1983, 120 pages, $6.

Training by Contract: College-Employer Profiles. As shown in these profiles, employers and colleges both benefit when an organization (such as business, government agency, and volunteer association) contracts directly with a college for the provision of instruction to its employees, clients, or members. (001753) 1983, 85 pages, $8.95.

To purchase books, see order form on next page.

College Board Publications
Department B23
Box 886
New York, New York 10101

Please send me the following titles:

Item number	Quan-tity	Title	Price	Subtotal (quantity × price)
╵_╵_╵_╵_╵_╵	___	_____	___	___
╵_╵_╵_╵_╵_╵	___	_____	___	___
╵_╵_╵_╵_╵_╵	___	_____	___	___
╵_╵_╵_╵_╵_╵	___	_____	___	___
╵_╵_╵_╵_╵_╵	___	_____	___	___
╵_╵_╵_╵_╵_╵	___	_____	___	___
╵_╵_╵_╵_╵_╵	___	_____	___	___
╵_╵_╵_╵_╵_╵	___	_____	___	___
╵_╵_╵_╵_╵_╵	___	_____	___	___
╵_╵_╵_╵_╵_╵	___	_____	___	___

Combined Subtotal _____

Calif. & Pa. residents add 6% sales tax _____

Total price $_____

Checks made payable to College Board must accompany all orders not submitted on an institutional purchase order, or the orders will be returned. *Orders for five or more copies of a single title receive a 20% discount unless quantity prices are listed.*

Name_____

Address_____

City_____State_____Zip_____

Prices are subject to change without notice.

Prepay orders under $10. Make checks payable to College Board. Postage will be charged for billed orders. Shipment will be made within 30 days of receipt of order. Mail this form to: **College Board Publications, Department B23, Box 886, New York, New York 10101.**

WITHDRAWN